# Blue Ribbon Commissions and Higher Education:
## Changing Academe from the Outside

by Janet Rogers-Clarke Johnson and Laurence R. Marcus

ASHE-ERIC Higher Education Report No. 2, 1986

*Prepared by*

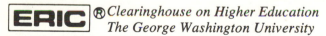 ® *Clearinghouse on Higher Education*
*The George Washington University*

*Published by*

*Association for the Study of Higher Education*

*Jonathan D. Fife,*
*Series Editor*

**Cite as**
Johnson, Janet R. and Marcus, Laurence R. *Blue Ribbon Commissions and Higher Education: Changing Academe from the Outside*. ASHE-ERIC Higher Education Report No. 2. Washington, D.C.: Association for the Study of Higher Education, 1986.

*Cover design by Michael David Brown, Inc., Rockville, MD.*

The ERIC Clearinghouse on Higher Education invites individuals to submit proposals for writing monographs for the Higher Education Report series. Proposals must include:
1. A detailed manuscript proposal of not more than five pages.
2. A 75-word summary to be used by several review committees for the initial screening and rating of each proposal.
3. A vita.
4. A writing sample.

**Library of Congress Catalog Card Number 86-71526**
**ISSN 0884-0040**
**ISBN 0-913317-29-2**

**ERIC®** **Clearinghouse on Higher Education**
The George Washington University
One Dupont Circle, Suite 630
Washington, D.C. 20036

**ASHE** **Association for the Study of Higher Education**
One Dupont Circle, Suite 630
Washington, D.C. 20036

This publication was partially prepared with funding from the Office of Educational Research and Improvement, U.S. Department of Education under contract no. 400-86-0017. The opinions expressed in this report do not necessarily reflect the positions or policies of OERI or the Department.

# EXECUTIVE SUMMARY

Leaders in the field of education at the national, state, and campus levels have wrestled over the past several decades with the question of how to develop the optimum kind of structure to address policy issues and concerns of higher education. A frequent technique or mechanism has been the use of blue ribbon commissions. Some blue ribbon commissions have been considered effective because they seem to have produced changes in higher education. However, many reports intended for use in planning have ended up on a shelf unused. This monograph includes a systematic review of blue ribbon commissions in the nation from 1965–1983 and looks at, among other facts, the number, purpose, authorizing bodies, composition, and recommendations of these commissions. It also includes an in-depth study of two blue ribbon commissions, the Rosenberg Commission in Maryland and the Wessell Commission in New York; explores the extent to which selected persons judge the use of blue ribbon commissions to be an effective vehicle for change in higher education; and considers what specific characteristics of blue ribbon commissions seem to be related to their effectiveness in terms of changes which can be attributed to the final commission reports.

## What Makes a Blue Ribbon Commission Effective?

The following factors appear to contribute to the effectiveness of a blue ribbon commission: attainability of commission objectives; adequacy of the amount of time allotted for the study; number of times commissioners meet; accessibility of commissioners to persons wishing to comment; sufficiency of the number of staff; selection of staff on the basis of merit alone; depth and breadth of background research conducted by staff; consideration of testimony from public hearings; favorable media reaction; repeated use of experts other than commission members and staff; ample substantiation of commission recommendations in the final report; consideration of the political potency of major affected interests in the implementation process; and the activity of the majority of commissioners in the implementation process.

## History of Blue Ribbon Commissions

Historically, the use of blue ribbon commissions in education is not an isolated or recent phenomenon. They occur at the national, state, and campus levels. Indeed, since 1929 there have been nearly 50 such commissions at the national level, and since 1965 there have been more than 50 blue ribbon commissions established at the state level.

Such commissions were established in the 1920s to investigate, plan, and assess higher education. At that time they tended to be concerned with broad policies. This outlook was modified during the 1940s and 1950s when special commissions were asked to help states focus on specific policy issues. During the 1960s blue ribbon commissions fell from favor. Critics suggested that such groups had only limited effectiveness since experts convened for a time to conduct a specific study inevitably were restricted in perspective, while the issues under investigation often were ongoing and bound to persist beyond the assigned time frame. Nonetheless, blue ribbon panels had great impact during this period as is apparent when one recognizes that the creation of numerous state coordinating boards was a product of special commissions. Although little has been written regarding the total number of these commissions and their effectiveness, their use has continued. Indeed, 25 states reported that between 1965 and 1983 either the governor or legislature had established at least one blue ribbon commission. Of these, 20 states had issued a broad charge to one or more of their respective commissions to explore issues such as access, enrollments, financing, student transfer policy, adult education, governance, program duplication, and long-range planning. This does not imply that special commissions are exclusively concerned with higher education. Special elementary/secondary commissions in recent years have addressed topics including accountability in schools, vocational education, school finances, the implementation of desegregation regulations, and general planning for the future.

**What Is a Blue Ribbon Commission?**
A blue ribbon commission has the following characteristics: (a) a predetermined life span; (b) eminent individuals from a variety of backgrounds; (c) staff and funds to assist in fulfilling its charge; (d) a charge to investigate and/or to recommend changes in structures, functions, origins, or processes. Such commissions have been charged to study and make recommendations on issues ranging from the

very narrow, such as the feasibility of establishing a branch campus, to very broad areas of concern, such as the improvement of the full range of educational opportunities in a state. They have been established also for the purpose of ameliorating an existing crisis situation.

**Are Blue Ribbon Commissions Useful on Campus?**
Campuses traditionally rely upon members of their own community to come together in ad hoc groups to attempt resolution on important issues. However, there are occasions where outside assistance is helpful and a blue ribbon panel might contribute. For example, campuses can become deeply divided over a specific issue, and a fresh view may be required to resolve the problem in a manner that will settle the immediate question and reduce (or eliminate) the level of rancor so that the campus might be united again. Another situation that calls for an outside panel of experts is when a college or university seeks to develop ties with, or expand its services to, a particular sector outside the institution. A third situation where a blue ribbon commission might be appropriate is when a college or university seeks to establish a planning agenda to move it to a position of leadership in a region or among institutions of similar size and mission.

**Blue Ribbon Commissions Criticized**
Certain criticisms have been leveled at the blue ribbon commission approach to planning and problem solving. Some criticisms allege that commissions tend to exaggerate the problems they address; that they draw broad and general conclusions rather than specific and adventurous conclusions; that their recommendations are beyond the financial means of those who would implement them; that they fail to spell out the details of their proposals; that they fail to document their proposed solutions.

While there may be some validity to these criticisms with regard to some blue ribbon commissions, the flaws are not universally true, nor are the criticisms irrefutable.

# ADVISORY BOARD

# CONSULTING EDITORS

**Richard Alfred**
Associate Professor and Chair
Graduate Program in Higher and Adult Continuing Education
University of Michigan

**Robert C. Andringa**
President
Creative Solutions

**Robert Atwell**
President
American Council on Education

**Robert Barak**
Deputy Executive Secretary
Director of Academic Affairs and Research
Iowa State Board of Regents

**John B. Bennett**
Director
Office on Self-Regulation
American Council on Education

**Larry Braskamp**
Assistant to the Vice Chancellor for Academic Affairs
University of Illinois

**Martin Finkelstein**
Associate Professor of Higher Education Administration
Seton Hall University

**Andrew T. Ford**
Provost and Dean of College
Allegheny College

**Mary Frank Fox**
Assistant Research Scientist
Center for Research on Social Organization
University of Michigan

**Timothy Gallineau**
Vice President for Student Development
Saint Bonaventure University

**G. Manuel Gunne**
Adjunct Associate Professor
College of Nursing
University of Utah

**W. Lee Hansen**
Professor
Department of Economics
University of Wisconsin

**L. Jackson Newell**
Professor and Dean
University of Utah

**Steven G. Olswang**
Assistant Provost for Academic Affairs
University of Washington

**Patricia Rueckel**
Executive Director
National Association for Women Deans,
    Administrators, and Counselors

**Richard F. Stevens**
Executive Director
National Association of Student Personnel Administrators

**James H. Werntz, Jr.**
Vice Chancellor for Academic Affairs
University of North Carolina

**Thomas R. Wolanin**
Staff Director
Subcommittee on Postsecondary Education
United States House of Representatives

# CONTENTS

# FOREWORD

Blue ribbon commissions are another tool in the decision-making arsenal, especially useful in providing impact and impetus for adopting new directions, formulating new ideas, and crystallizing long-range goals. The use of blue ribbon commissions will undoubtedly increase in the next 20 years, keeping pace with the increasing conflict within institutions as major issues that are at the heart of institutional stability become threatened. The basic scenario is familiar: the lack of personnel turnover may lead to a stagnation of ideas, while steady enrollment figures and stable government funding keep the monetary pie the same size. Adjusting to new student interests and workforce demands means new programs will have to be funded at the expense of old ones. Even as higher education moves into a period of relative financial stability, recent general commission reports and study groups on higher education have heightened its visibility and therefore public expectations and demands for greater accountability. As new expectations receive publicity, so too the failure to meet these expectations increases discontentment.

Enter the blue ribbon commission. Blue ribbon commissions are highly visible and usually broad-based, drawing experts from across the educational spectrum. They are especially useful for making decisions on large policy issues, doubly so when the action to be taken could prove to be unpopular. Many upcoming issues will benefit from consideration by a large number of experts than generally reside within a single administration. Blue ribbon commissions can usually insure that issues are deliberated fairly and in-depth, long-range recommendations are responsive and responsible, and critical decisions are arrived at in an objective manner. These features make blue ribbon commissions highly attractive to administrators facing critical decisions that affect the institution as a whole.

One key to successful decision making is to identify the particular group of individuals, inside or outside the institution, who can assist the leadership in a careful consideration of pertinent data. This report, written by Janet Rogers-Clarke Johnson, senior research associate at the Educational Testing Service, and Laurence Marcus, director of the Office for State Colleges in the New Jersey Department of Higher Education, reviews the general process adopted by large external panels referred to as blue ribbon commissions. The report also examines in-depth two particular panels—the Wessell and Rosenberg Commissions—in an effort to identify characteristics that lead to success or failure. The authors further relate how these types of panels have been and can be used at the individual campus level. Understanding the effectiveness of blue ribbon commissions at the national and state levels will help administrators understand when and how to resort to blue ribbon commissions at the campus level.

Every forward-looking institution craves new ideas, new directions, and new solutions to problems. Responsible department chairs and deans alike seek new decision-making tools. The model of the blue ribbon commission contains elements that can be applied to issues of limited scope, such as those within a single school or even a department. After reading this report, administrators will have gleaned useful information for attacking old problems with new vigor.

**Jonathan D. Fife**
Series Editor
Professor and Director
ERIC Clearinghouse on Higher Education
The George Washington University

# INTRODUCTION

Higher education is confronted with a unique planning challenge: how to do more with less. If this were the result of a sour economy, the challenge would not be so unique. There would be a general expectation that when times got better finances would improve. This, however, is not the case. Growing concern about such conditions as declining enrollments, increased financial stringency, and accountability have induced various interest groups, such as faculty, trustees, state agency personnel, governors, and legislators, to consider numerous strategies for the planning, review, and evaluation of the effectiveness of higher education and its delivery system in the light of continuing cutbacks. These strategies for planning include employing consultants from inside as well as outside the state, calling upon legislative and executive task forces, forming permanent statewide planning boards either by statute or, in some cases, by state constitutions, and appointing blue ribbon commissions. It is important to these top state and educational leaders to know the potential worth and limit of the blue ribbon commission approach to policy development in higher education. These special commissions continue to be used as a vehicle to study the situation of postsecondary education, and to make responsible recommendations for its future development. The ongoing dynamics of postsecondary education and the continual need for reevaluation and assessment occasioned by changing conditions seem to indicate a likelihood that more special study groups will be created at the national, state, and campus levels.

*Higher education is confronted with a unique planning challenge: how to do more with less.*

## Blue Ribbon Commissions

Blue ribbon commissions are a frequent vehicle for the examination of complex problems. They occur at the national, state, and campus levels. Indeed, since 1929 there have been nearly 50 such commissions at the national level alone. Blue ribbon commissions also are applicable at the campus level and a number of institutions have begun to take this approach, most recently Rutgers, the State University of New Jersey. Colleges and universities traditionally have used standing committees or special task forces to address important issues. Sometimes external consultants are called in to assist, usually by providing an objective, professional review and opinion. In the same vein, blue ribbon commissions can be a useful approach on campus especially in instances where an issue has divided sentiment across a campus, or when a college or university wants to develop ties with a particular sector outside of the institution. Another situation where a blue ribbon commission might be appropriate is when a college or university seeks to establish a planning agenda intended to move it to a position of leadership in a region or among institutions of similar size and mission. Blue ribbon commissions also are useful planning tools when institutions are negotiating broad strategies for interaction. Blue ribbon commissions also have been utilized to make recommendations concerning planning and coordination in multicampus settings.

Certainly, blue ribbon commissions on the campus (and variations involving external persons alongside institutional personnel) have made positive contributions. They do not take away from traditional decision-making processes on campus; rather they add to them by providing equally professional and responsible, but detached, views.

**Blue Ribbon Commission Defined**
Embodied in the "President's Commission on Campus Unrest" are a number of elements which help to define a blue ribbon commission: (1) it was established to study a specific problem; (2) its existence was of fixed duration; (3) it was composed of eminent individuals from a variety of backgrounds; (4) it was provided with a staff and funds to assist in fulfilling its charge.

# MOBILIZING NATIONAL OPINION

Blue ribbon commissions are intended to make news. They also are intended to make things happen. The report of the National Commission on Excellence in Education (1983) illustrates this dramatically for the field of education. In recent years SAT scores have been declining; huge numbers of students have been performing poorly on basic skills examinations; colleges have launched major remedial efforts; employers have been complaining about the inability of their young employees to demonstrate proficiency in fundamental areas. Yet it took the report of a group of eminent Americans commissioned by the Secretary of Education to drive home the point that something had gone afoul in our schools. As the commission put it: "If an unfriendly foreign power had attempted to impose on America the mediocre educational performance that exists today, we might have viewed it as an act of war" (p. 5). America's collective ears perked up. For the first time since 1957, when Russia launched its first sputnik, concern for the quality of education captured the nation's attention. Without doubt, the report of the Commission on Excellence is responsible for this concern.

### National Advisory Committee on Education
Historically, the use of blue ribbon commissions is not an isolated or recent phenomenon. Such commissions were established as far back as the 1920s as a strategy for producing constructive change in the overall planning of education as well as in specific issue areas. The commissions at that time tended to be concerned with broad policies. For example, President Herbert Hoover appointed a National Advisory Committee on Education in 1929 to study the federal role in education, an area historically reserved to the states. The committee's report, "Federal Relations to Education," released two years later, called upon the federal government to provide general financial support for education, to cease categorical aid programs, and to end requirements that states provide matching funds in order to use federal money (p. 31). Thus, the report proposed the abolition of any federal control over funds disbursed to the states for educational purposes in the belief that local educational autonomy was the source of America's political virility.

*The political domination of education by a remote central government . . . has always led to the evils of bureaucratic unresponsiveness to local and changing needs, to bureaucratic standardization, red tape and delay, and to official insensitiveness to the criticism of far-distant parents and citizens* (National Advisory Committee on Education 1931, p. 29).

Members agreed that local control of education provides protection against totalitarianism:

*A class or party may capture a central government by revolution or by some exigency of politics; it cannot as readily capture 48 states and more than 145,000 local school communities* (National Advisory Committee on Education 1931, p. 37).

Nevertheless, the committee worried that "the federal government has no conclusive and consistent public policy" on what it should do in the field of education. It recommended that the time had come to establish a cabinet-level education department with "an educational officer of equal status with the heads of all other departments" in order to "integrate the educational resources of the government" (National Advisory Committee on Education 1931, pp. 94–107).

However, a cabinet-level U.S. Department of Education was not established until the presidency of Jimmy Carter, and block grants were not available to education until the presidency of Ronald Reagan. Even then block grants had many more strings than the committee suggested in 1931. In other words, not every blue ribbon commission produces an immediate result.

**Nationally Oriented Blue Ribbon Commissions**
In recent years a number of nationally oriented blue ribbon commissions have focused on higher education. For example, in the aftermath of the 1970 shooting of students at Kent State University by Ohio National Guardsmen and at Jackson State College by Mississippi State Police, President Richard M. Nixon established the President's Commission on Campus Unrest. Its goals were "to identify the principal causes of campus violence" that had character-

ized the late 1960s and had exploded after the American invasion of Cambodia in the spring of 1970; to determine why ''the processes for orderly expression of dissent'' had broken down; to recommend a process for the resolution of legitimate grievances on campus; and

*to suggest ways to protect and enhance the right of academic freedom, the right to pursue an education free from improper interference and the right of peaceful dissent and protest* (Scranton 1970, p. 535).

Former Pennsylvania Governor William W. Scranton chaired the nine-member panel. It had a staff of 139, and in three months, it held 13 public hearings and met 15 times in executive session. It concluded:

*Too many Americans have begun to justify violence as a means of effecting change or safeguarding traditions. Too many have forgotten the values and sense of shared humanity that unite us. Campus violence reflects this national condition* (Scranton 1970, p. 1).

The commission found that campus violence was a factor of racial injustice, the war in Southeast Asia, and the policies of the university. Members urged a return to our tradition of tolerance and called for a national reconciliation. At the core of this plea for national unity was a recommendation for an end to the Vietnam War, a renewal of the national commitment to full social justice, and reform of the university (Scranton 1970, pp. 3,6,9).

As history documents, it was some time before the war ended, and our nation has yet to return to its early 1960s commitment to full social justice. But there has been major reform among our colleges and universities. In part, this was a factor of the Commission on Campus Unrest and of subsequent national panels.

Nixon's Health, Education, and Welfare Secretary, Robert Finch, formed a task force of educators to examine the problems confronting higher education as it entered the 1970s. The ''Report on Higher Education'' (1971) spoke of the need for higher education to open its door to new populations—older students, minorities, and women—and of the desirability of transforming federal financial aid grants so that money goes to the student who chooses which institution to attend, rather than to the institutions which choose the students to give it to. It also suggested the establishment of regional examining universities which could grant credit and degrees for collegiate-level knowledge gained by persons outside of the college setting. It also put forth a radical hypothesis—that "dropping out" of college need not be an indication of failure and need not be irrevocable (Newman 1971).

### Carnegie Commission

The six-year study of the Carnegie Commission on Higher Education reinforced much that the Newman Report said. The commission produced 21 reports and 85 studies and technical reports before issuing its final report, "Priorities for Action"(1973). By looking beyond the role of colleges and universities in the creation and transmission of knowledge, the Carnegie Commission called upon them to assist in the advancement of social change by promoting equal opportunity through admissions, hiring, research, and service.

The commission also spoke of the need for reforms regarding curriculum, attendance patterns, institutional quality, and so forth. It concluded that the single most important issue regarding change was "whether it will be imposed more totally from external sources" and argued for

> *presidents who will give forward-looking leadership, for increased input from student sources into decision-making processes, for effective boards of trustees, and for the releasing of individual faculty initiative from undue prior restraints* (Carnegie 1973, p. 51).

The Newman and Carnegie reports provided the impetus for great change in higher education. Most reforms were not forced from the outside but came from within. Without question, there were other forces (i.e., the Vietnam War, the impending decline in the number of college students of traditional age, federal affirmative action mandates, etc.) that came into play. However, educators often move slowly and not without the support of other educators. Faculty and students concerned about social justice and

curricular reform were buoyed by the proposals of Newman and Carnegie, both the result of studies by prestigious
educators.

## Governance Issues

Periods of great change are often followed by stocktaking.
Such was the case by the end of the 1970s when many
educators were voicing concern over the regulation which
was accompanying federal and state funds (Marcus,
Leone, and Goldberg 1983, pp. 12–14). To many, it
appeared as if the decisions driving higher education were
no longer being made on the campus—the very specter
that the Carnegie Commission hoped to avoid when it
reported earlier in the decade. Two major blue ribbon studies sought to address this concern.

The first was formed in 1977 by the Alfred P. Sloan
Foundation, which cited the need for

> *a detailed, comprehensive analysis of the regulatory pro-*
> *cess by a distinguished but disinterested body whose rec-*
> *ommendations would define and protect—and would be*
> *seen to define and protect—the public interest* (Sloan
> Commission on Government and Higher Education 1980,
> p. xi).

The commission was charged to answer the following questions:

> *How does the country strike the balance between institu-*
> *tional freedom and government authority? To what ex-*
> *tent is the academic institution to be responsive to what*
> *may be perceived as social needs?* (Sloan 1980, p. xi).

Composed of educators, corporate leaders, journalists
and persons with high-level government experience, the
Sloan Commission presented a balanced report which concluded that "government enforcement of laws and regulations encroaches on decisions held to be central to the traditional autonomy of the academic world," but that higher
education "cannot consistently call for less government
and more [public] money at the same time" (pp. 36–37). It
found federal civil rights enforcement efforts to be burden-
some to higher education, resulting too often in litigation.

However, it noted that "more than good intentions" by colleges and universities are necessary, and thus, that "sanctions and controls must be maintained," but through a proposed independent regulatory agency to be known as the Council for Equal Opportunity in Higher Education and to be housed within the new U.S. Department of Education (pp. 9–12).

The commission handled the matter of quality control efforts by state governments in a similar manner.

*Any governmental effort, whether state or federal, to evaluate the quality of education arouses profound uneasiness throughout the higher education community. It is seen as a threat to institutional autonomy and academic freedom* (Sloan 1980, p. 16).

Nevertheless, the commission concluded that the possibility of declining academic standards as a response to a declining pool of students was great enough to justify "so radical a step" as to have each state arrange for a "periodic review of the quality of educational programs at every public college and university" within the state. These reviews were to be conducted by academic peer groups, not state employees. It also noted that private institutions should be included in the review process since "it is more likely that wasteful duplication of programs could be avoided and that contraction of capacity would proceed as equitably as possible" (Sloan 1980, pp. 16–17).

The same concerns which prompted the creation of the Sloan Commission also led the Carnegie Foundation for the Advancement of Learning to establish a National Panel on Government and Higher Education. Its 1982 report was not as even-handed. While deploring "the suspicion and lack of trust that has sometimes been revealed by both academics and government officials," the report paints government as the heavy. It concluded that "[a]s public officials introduce more and more oversight requirements, the process becomes overburdened, contradictory, and finally incoherent," and warned that the imposition of "suffocating requirements on colleges at a time when flexibility is required is the wrong prescription." The report asserted "that the most serious problem encountered by higher education is the cumulative impact of government interven-

tion'' (Carnegie 1982, pp. 44, 62, 67). Its recommended
reforms were couched in that light.

**Commissions Bring Insight to Perplexing Problems**
This discussion of nationally focused blue ribbon commissions is not intended to be exhaustive but to cite examples
of the frequent resort to the ''distinguished but disinterested body'' to bring insights into some perplexing problems. These illustrations show the variety in breadth,
depth, timeliness, and controversy possible among blue
ribbon commissions. Some, such as the Newman Commission and the Carnegie Commission, help to get a consensus
that facilitates change. Others, such as the 1929 National
Advisory Committee on Education, make recommendations that are not realized until years later. While it is still
too early to judge the impact of the reports of the Sloan
Commission and the National Panel on Government and
Higher Education, one can hypothesize that their diver-
gence in tone, if not view, is representative of a rift too raw
to be resolved quickly.

# STATE-LEVEL COMMISSIONS

For the last several decades, institutions of higher learning have squared off with state coordinating agencies to create an equipoise on matters of long-range planning. As the state agency would have the process work, it would establish the statewide planning direction and the individual institutions would develop plans accordingly. The colleges and universities, holding dearly to their traditions of independence, would have the statewide plan be a reflection of the composite of individual institutional views. In most instances, acceptable compromises result. However, on occasion even the best functioning planning processes are inadequate to address issues of urgency, particularly when they concern such matters as the fundamental relationships between government and higher education, institutional finance, response to broad societal changes having an impact on institutional mission and student access, or the overall governance of higher education within a state. In such cases, decision makers have turned to blue ribbon commissions as a strategy for producing constructive change.

The decision to use the blue ribbon commission approach to planning or issue resolution is not arrived at randomly. The conditions facing higher education today are very severe. Declining enrollments, decreasing fiscal resources and appropriations, continuing performance as well as fiscal audits, and demands for accountability are just a few of the concerns reflected in the charges assigned to blue ribbon commissions. These commissions are a consciously decided upon strategy to cope and to plan.

Indeed, the shift in the role of state government regarding education and the changing profile of state legislatures is creating a trend toward greater reliance on specialized committees. Also, most states are confronted at some time with the need to address controversial issues of education policy in a highly visible environment. In such cases, the creation of a respected, blue ribbon commission is frequently a successful strategy.

In order to understand the importance and use of blue ribbon commissions in state planning for higher education, and how these commissions represent a kind of interface between the task of statewide coordinating/governing bodies and legislatures, it is desirable to place them in context by means of an overview of state planning methods, state-

*. . . Most states are confronted at some time with the need to address controversial issues of education policy in a highly visible environment.*

wide coordination and the role of state government. A comprehensive overview of state blue ribbon commissions established across the country from 1965 to 1983 will be provided.

### State-Level Blue Ribbon Commission Defined

State-level blue ribbon commissions have the same characteristics enumerated earlier for national panels. A blue ribbon commission requires persons from a variety of backgrounds; this excludes a number of state-level panels that might be characterized by some as "blue ribbon." For example, study commissions composed solely of legislators, or solely of members of the state board of higher education, are not included. Further, since we are interested in groups with official standing, our consideration is limited to blue ribbon commissions that have been gubernatorially or legislatively appointed, or that have been empanelled by the state higher education coordinating board. Commissions established by foundations or by groups of corporate leaders are not included.

A blue ribbon commission, like any special committee or task force, is established for a purpose. Usually this purpose is spelled out in the charge given to the commission by the establishing authority, e.g. the legislature or governor, and this explicit charge can range from the very broad to the very specific. However, the explicit and publicly stated charge issued to a commission may be telling only part of the real story. Increasingly, the issues are complex and politically sensitive. Rarely in the 1980s are commissions set up to decide growth issues like how to expand the higher education system in a given state. Instead, systems and institutions are considering alternatives designed to contract the enterprise, such as closing programs and merging institutions. Changes in this direction do not come about easily or without raised voices, and ultimately some perceived unfavorable outcomes by some group or other.

Thus, while the public charge to a commission can simply outline the issues to be investigated, usually much more is at stake and a commission can be consciously established for a variety of additional, unspoken reasons. These can include balancing the biases surrounding politically sensitive issues through commissioner selection, as well as sometimes stacking the balance through the same means.

State-level blue ribbon commissions have been established to address very specific issues or concerns. In 1976, the Arizona Legislature authorized a special commission "to make a preliminary investigation of all facets involved in the establishment and operation of a branch campus of Arizona State University on the west side of Maricopa County" (Whiteman 1977, p. 1). Blue ribbon commissions also have been issued broad charges. Such was the case in Florida in 1970, for example, when the Legislature requested a commission "to prepare and submit . . . its report and recommendations for coordination and furtherance of all types of education beyond high school" (Graham 1970, p. v.).

The composition of special commissions can vary. Since 1965, Alaska, California, Connecticut, Iowa, Louisiana, Nebraska, North Dakota, Tennessee, and Vermont have reported commissions made up exclusively of legislators. Commissions whose membership represents a combination of lay persons and legislators include Arizona, Ohio, Massachusetts, Texas, and Wisconsin. In Alabama, Arizona, California, Florida, Michigan, Mississippi, Vermont, and Washington, commissions included educators, lay persons and/or legislators. Wholly lay membership constituted the 1977 Commission on the Future of Education in Delaware. Some states utilized the services of special consulting firms to conduct a special study. These firms contracted directly with the state government or agency to prepare all or part of a report in Alaska, Florida, Mississippi, North Dakota, and West Virginia. The blue ribbon commission itself contracted with them in Maine.

Lyman Glenny studied the use of planning teams made up of in-state experts and volunteers (1967, p. 3). He brought together a variety of persons intimately acquainted with a state's educational history and institutions, as well as the state's politics and power structure, and found that dialogue is encouraged between interest groups who initially may not be predisposed to one another's viewpoints. The investment of educators and citizens provides commitment, and thus a foundation, for the acceptance of final recommendations. Involving a large number of persons provides a greater opportunity for enriched discussion upon which judgments may be made; more so than is feasible with a limited number of professional consultants who might have been assembled to study the same problem.

Such committees should include persons representative of interest groups that take a public stance on education issues. A broad range of participation in formulating plans or recommendations invites the expression and consideration of a variety of opinions and concerns, and generally results in a better plan with a greater chance of societal acceptance. During the formulation period, it is extremely important to be in close communication with institutions, the public, and political leaders. Without open communication channels, the chances of final implementation of the plan are greatly reduced (Glenny et al. 1971, p. 34).

*It is the planning process, the kinds of people involved, and the leadership throughout the planning period that ultimately determine whether the plan is understood, is politically acceptable, and can be implemented as designed.* (Glenny et al. 1971, p. 34).

Further, the involvement of persons representative of interest groups in the recommending process will facilitate communication between the planning agency and the general public. This communication is especially important at the time of legislative adoption of the implementing statutes.

Historically, the state use of blue ribbon commissions is not an isolated or recent phenomenon. Such commissions were established in the 1920s to investigate, plan, and assess higher education. At that time, they tended to be concerned with broad policies. This outlook was modified during the 1940s and 1950s when special commissions were asked to help states focus on specific policy issues. During the 1960s, blue ribbon commissions fell from favor. Critics suggested that such groups had only limited effectiveness since experts convened for a time to conduct a specific study inevitably were restricted in perspective, whereas the issues under investigation often were ongoing and bound to persist beyond the assigned time frame (Johnson 1982, p. 1). However, blue ribbon commissions were still used and many of the 24 statewide boards established during this period were a product of special commissions (Millard 1977, p. 26). Blue ribbon commissions continue to be used, and used effectively, to examine a wide range of state education policy questions. For example, between 1965 and 1983, 25 states created at least one commission specifically concerned with issues of higher education. This does not imply that special commissions are exclusively concerned with higher education. Special elementary/secondary commissions in recent years have addressed topics including accountability in schools, vocational education, school finance, the implementation of desegregation regulations, and general planning for the future. Some commissions have researched these topics in conjunction with higher education issues. Results have ranged from formal implementation of commission recommendations in new legislation to informal placing of a topic on a state's policy agenda (Burnes et al. 1983, p. 2).

**Resorting to Blue Ribbon Commissions**
Major impact is most likely to occur when proposed reforms can develop consensus; that is, when proposals are readily understandable, are the obvious next step, and do not require a movement away from a basic principle. Problems that are more likely to fall into this category are commonly the focus of study by state-level commissions. For example, between 1960 and 1975, 24 statewide higher education coordinating or governing boards were established; many were the direct result of blue ribbon studies focused on the issue of managing higher education growth (Millard 1977, p. 26). Many states have relied frequently on the blue ribbon commission approach to resolve a variety of problems.

Using New Jersey as an example, seven panels have focused on higher education since 1965: the Citizens Committee for Higher Education in New Jersey (1965) led to the creation of the Board of Higher Education, the upgrading of the state teachers' colleges into comprehensive arts and sciences colleges with professional programs, the creation of boards of trustees for these colleges, and the general expansion of the higher education system (Goheen 1965, pp. 14–16). The Commission on Financing Postsecondary Education (1974) led to policies setting tuition as a fixed percentage of the cost of education at public colleges and universities, and to a single statewide, need-based tuition aid grant program geared to tuition charges in the various sectors of higher education (Booher 1977, pp. 11–12). The Commission to Study the Mission, Financing and Governance of the County Colleges (1978) led to the removal of elected officials from county college trustee boards, to the placement of two state-appointed trustees on those boards, and to an increase in the state's share of county college budgets (Taylor 1979, pp. 10–12); The Commission to Study Teacher Preparation Programs in New Jersey Colleges (1978)—a group established by the Legislature—led to a restructuring of teacher education programs around a solid general education core and a major in an arts and sciences discipline (Johnson 1981, p. viii). The Blue Ribbon Panel on Teacher Education (1981) led to specific guidelines implementing the recommendations of the aforementioned group established by the Legislature (Berg 1981, pp. 3–4). The Commission on the Future of the State Colleges (1982) was established to examine issues of state college mission, governance and financing. The Governor's Commission on Science and Technology, (1982) was established in 1982, to identify those research and development areas that should be enhanced in the state's research universities in order to enhance the state's economy. The latter two commissions issued reports in early 1984.

Seven commissions in New Jersey in less than two decades indicate the reliance that state policy makers place on this approach. Commissions were appointed by two different governors, the Legislature and the chancellor of higher education, as well as by the Board of Higher Education on three different occasions.

**Increased Activity by State Government**

The growing sophistication of data gathering and management techniques, of budgeting procedures, and of the staffs involved in state agencies prompts state governments (governors, legislatures, and state agencies) to conduct their own in-depth analyses, to review statewide systems of education, and even to review the appropriation requests and program planning of individual institutions. These activities are motivated by the large financial contribution made by the state to education coupled with a certain lack of faith on the side of state government in the institutional ability to plan effectively and efficiently for the expenditure of state appropriations (Johnson 1982, p. 7).

The character of state legislatures has been changing over the last decade in capacity, internal distribution of power, habits of work and composition (Rosenthal 1977, p. 2). An increase in capacity is due to an increase in the size of legislative staff and their increasing professionalism (Oregon Legislative Research 1973, p. 1). The use of staffs of specialists allows for more areas of expertise and more sophisticated analysis that help the legislature deal with a growing and complex number of issues. The internal power structure has evolved from a strong centralized leadership to a more fragmented structure occasioned by heavier reliance on standing committees. In conjunction with their staff, these committees are developing policies and programs for legislative consideration. It is the standing committee on education, for example, that is the focal point for in-depth investigation and deliberation, instead of the older style of more general discussion in the full legislature.

Another group wielding substantial power within state government is the governor's budget staff. This staff joins the ranks of those state level groups described as the "anonymous leaders of higher education" (Glenny 1972, p. 18). The blue ribbon commission is a specialized planning mechanism and can satisfy an executive or a legislature that its intervention is not necessary. In fact, many commissions are established by governors and legislatures precisely to preclude any perception of partisan response in an area which most people believe should be free of partisanship.

### Overview of Blue Ribbon Commissions: 1965–1983
A survey of states initiated in 1979 ascertained among other facts the number, purpose, authorizing bodies, composition, and recommendations of blue ribbon commissions set up across the country between 1965 and 1979 (J. Johnson 1982). Prior to this survey, no nationwide analysis of information on such special commissions existed. The following data are based primarily on the original survey updated by information received from the governance center of the Education Commission of the States in 1983 and subject to certain limits of the state update. Several commissions have concluded their studies since the initial col-

lection of updated data and this report were done. Also, not all states provided information on commissions between 1979 and 1983. The reports of blue ribbon commissions analyzed and referenced in this study are listed in the bibliography. The reports are placed in alphabetical order usually by the name of the commission chairperson.

Forty-three states responded with information on blue ribbon commissions set up in their states between 1965 and 1983. Eight states reported that no blue ribbon commissions were established in that period (see Table 1).

### Table 1
### STATES REPORTING NO BLUE RIBBON COMMISSIONS BETWEEN 1965 AND 1983

| | |
|---|---|
| Arkansas | New Mexico |
| Hawaii | Oklahoma |
| Idaho | Pennsylvania |
| Minnesota | West Virginia |

Twenty-five states reported having had one or more blue ribbon commissions. States in which the legislature exclusively conducted a special study, either by its own members or by contract with a professional research organization (see Table 2), do not qualify since the composition of the special study commission/committee does not represent a mix of individuals from a variety of backgrounds.

### TABLE 2
### STATES IN WHICH THE LEGISLATURE CONDUCTED A SPECIAL STUDY EITHER BY ITS OWN MEMBERS OR BY CONTRACT WITH A PROFESSIONAL RESEARCH ORGANIZATION 1965–1983*

| | |
|---|---|
| *Alaska | Nebraska |
| California | North Dakota |
| Connecticut | Tennessee |
| Illinois | Vermont |
| *Iowa | *West Virginia |
| Louisiana | |

*These studies are not classified as blue ribbon commissions because they do not satisfy all our definitional criteria.
*Denotes those states which contracted with a professional research organization.

In 11 states special studies were undertaken at the instigation of the statewide coordinating agency; in California and Wisconsin, the statewide agency was requested to prepare a study by either the legislature or the governor (see Table 3).

### TABLE 3

**STATES IN WHICH THE STATEWIDE COORDINATING AGENCY WAS RESPONSIBLE FOR A SPECIAL STUDY 1965–1983\***

| | |
|---|---|
| Alabama | Ohio |
| California | Oregon |
| Illinois | Rhode Island |
| Kentucky | Texas |
| New Jersey | Wisconsin |
| North Dakota | |

\*These studies are not classified as blue ribbon commissions because they do not satisfy all our definitional criteria.

A variety of additional configurations were employed by states to study or explore postsecondary issues. For example, Ohio has a Governor's Council for Cost Control that is a non-profit corporation organized and financed by the state's private sector. This council has undertaken several studies concerned with higher education.

In 25 states the governor or the legislature established blue ribbon commissions between 1965 and 1983 as listed in Table 4 (p. 20). Sixteen states, or 64 per cent of those reporting blue ribbon commissions established and appointed by either the governor or legislature between 1965 and 1983, have had more than one blue ribbon commission. In eight states, such an approach was taken more than once in a five-year period.

Of the 25 states reporting gubernatorially or legislatively established ribbon commissions, 20 states issued a broad charge to one or more of their respective commissions to explore issues such as access, enrollments, financing, student transfer policy, adult education, governance, program duplication and long-range planning. In short, these commissions were charged to review the state postsecondary education system and to recommend changes. (Other commissions had more narrowly defined charges focused on such issues as teacher education or high technology.)

# TABLE 4

## STATES CONDUCTING GUBERNATORIALLY OR LEGISLATIVELY ESTABLISHED BLUE RIBBON COMMISSION STUDIES BETWEEN 1965 AND 1983

| State | Year | Authorized By | Broadly Charged |
|---|---|---|---|
| Alabama | 1968 | Legislature | X |
| | 1977 | Lieutenant Governor | X |
| Arizona | 1976 | Legislature | |
| California | 1978 | Governor | X |
| Connecticut | 1971 | Governor | X |
| | 1976 | Governor | X |
| | 1981 | Governor | X |
| Delaware | 1976 | Governor | X |
| | 1977 | Governor | X |
| Florida | 1970 | Legislature (appointed by governor) | X |
| | 1973 | Governor | |
| | 1980 | Legislature (appointed by both legislature and governor) | X |
| Georgia | 1982 | Governor | X |
| Illinois | 1976 | Governor | |
| Indiana | 1965 | Governor | |
| | 1967 | General Assembly | X |
| | 1969 | Governor | |
| | 1971 | Governor | X |
| Iowa | 1969 | Governor | X |
| | 1979 | Governor | X |
| Maine | 1966 | Legislature (appointed by governor) | X |
| | 1973 | Legislature (2 members to be appointed by the legislature; 11 members to be appointed by governor) | |

TABLE 4 (continued)

| State | Year | Authorized By | Broadly Charged |
|-------|------|---------------|:---------------:|
| Maryland | 1975 | Governor | X |
| Michigan | 1974 | Governor | X |
| Mississippi | 1974 | Governor | X |
| Missouri | 1970 | Governor | |
| | 1978 | Governor (6 members appointed by legislature) | |
| Montana | 1974 | Governor | X |
| New Jersey | 1965 | Governor | |
| | 1978 | Legislature | |
| | 1982 | Governor | |
| New York | 1968 | Governor | |
| | 1973 | Governor | |
| | 1976 | Governor | |
| North Carolina | 1971 | Governor | X |
| | 1983 | Governor | X |
| North Dakota | 1982 | Legislature | X |
| Tennessee | 1971 | Governor | X |
| | 1982 | Legislature | |
| Texas | 1977 | Legislature (9 members appointed by governor) | X |
| | 1982 | Governor | X |
| Vermont | 1969 | Governor | |
| | 1973 | Governor | X |
| Washington | 1969 | Legislature (some members appointed by governor) | X |
| | 1982 | Legislature | X |
| Wisconsin | 1968 | Governor | |
| | 1970 | Governor | X |
| | 1976 | Governor | |

**Recommendations of Blue Ribbon Commissions**

Since the literature on the work of the blue ribbon commissions is rather sparse, the various commission reports can serve as the basis for further analysis. Having already looked at the frequency of their use and who appointed them, it is appropriate now to consider the outcomes of the state-level blue ribbon commissions. Since the commissions usually were given a broad charge, the recommendations cover a wide variety of areas (see Table 5).

TABLE 5

AREAS IN WHICH BLUE RIBBON COMMISSIONS
MADE RECOMMENDATIONS

| Area | Number of Commissions | Number of States |
|---|---|---|
| Academic Quality | 2 | 2 |
| Articulation | 2 | 2 |
| Branch or New Campus | 4 | 4 |
| Budgeting Procedures | 2 | 2 |
| Continuing Education | 2 | 2 |
| Create or Strengthen State Agency | 15 | 11 |
| Data Collection | 3 | 3 |
| Financing Institutions | 6 | 6 |
| Financial Aid | 7 | 7 |
| Governance | 9 | 8 |
| Master Planning | 7 | 6 |
| Medical or Health Education | 6 | 5 |
| Operational Efficiency | 3 | 2 |
| Private Institutions | 2 | 2 |
| Teacher Education | 1 | 1 |

*Creation or Strengthening of State Higher Education Agency*
The growth of higher education in the 1960s to accommodate the post–World War II baby boom generation and the challenges of the economic downturn of the 1970s gave rise to the creation of a number of state higher education agencies and to the broadening of others. Fifteen commissions in 11 states made recommendations regarding the establishment or strengthening of state agencies during the period under study (see Table 5). This was, by far, the single most important focus of activity of the blue ribbon commissions.

## Governance Issues

In all sections of the country in the 1970s, states were rethinking the governance of public institutions of higher education. Making recommendations in this area was a priority of blue ribbon commissions and marked a change from the preceding decade. Following the rapid growth of their higher education systems in the 1960s, states recognized the need for establishing structures to oversee public institutions. Nine commissions in eight states debated such questions as who was to control state institutions of higher education, and who should make decisions (See Table 5). Their recommendations varied depending on individual needs and responsibilities. Connecticut (1971) and Vermont (1973) recommended a single governing board for all public institutions of higher education. Michigan (1974), New Jersey (1978), and Washington (1969) addressed the question of the best method of selecting members for the boards of trustees of their institutions. Montana (1974) recommended that the effectiveness of governance patterns be reviewed every five years.

*Following the rapid growth of . . . the 1960s, states recognized the need for establishing structures to oversee public institutions.*

## Expansion of Higher Education

Numerous commissions spoke directly to the need to expand higher educational opportunities within the state. A review of commission reports indicates the complexity of problems faced by the states, and how each commission tried to tailor its recommendations to practical needs. In Indiana, for instance, the state stood in need of expanding opportunities for public medical education. An Indiana commission (1969) recommended establishing seven medical education centers to be operated in conjunction with the state's major universities.

Another approach to expansion, favored by Arizona (1976) Florida (1970), and Washington (1969), was to establish new public colleges or branch campuses. Other commissions sought to make use of the capacity and plants of private colleges. In Missouri (1970) and Washington (1969), commissions recommended that the expenses of state residents be subsidized at independent institutions within the state through a contract between the state and participating colleges. Several commissions, including Mississippi (1974), Maine (1973), and New Jersey (1974), recommended developing or expanding student financial aid programs as a means of expanding access to higher education.

*Master Planning*

Commissions in California (1971 and 1973), Florida (1970), Kansas (1970), Kentucky (1981), Maine (1966), and Montana (1974) either developed, reviewed, or evaluated statewide master plans for higher education. The "Final Report of the Montana Commission on Postsecondary Education" was so comprehensive that it deserves special mention (James 1974). Its recommendations included many areas found in Table 5.

Established by the governor, this 30-member panel was asked to make a detailed study of postsecondary education in Montana with specific attention given to inventories of postsecondary educational resources, accountability, planning and coordination, and access for all persons who desired and could benefit from postsecondary education. Its report included 127 recommendations, many proposing procedures of a rather detailed nature.

In addition to areas commonly found in comprehensive plans (the need for enhanced funding, more student financial aid, broadened access, planning for new programs, and so forth), the Montana Commission provided a set of recommendations intended to enhance the educational opportunities available to native Americans and to expand programs for the study of Indian culture. The report also contained recommendations which may be common policy issues now, but which were not so common in 1974. For example, the commission recommended that all Montana residents 62 years of age and over have tuition-free access on a space available basis to all courses in the university system. It also recommended the development of a voluntary early retirement program for full-time faculty, as well as the establishment of childcare facilities at all colleges and universities (James 1974).

The members of the Montana Commission obviously believed that the state would benefit from the future use of blue ribbon commissions. They recommended that every eight years an 11-member lay panel be appointed by the governor to review the condition of higher education and to conduct a long-range study.

## Special Circumstances

In addition to blue ribbon commissions charged to focus on broad issues, other commissions were given a narrower charge to fit special circumstances. For example, the Arizona legislature established a four-member Medical School Admissions Review Committee in 1972 for a specific purpose: to review the admissions practices and policies of the College of Medicine at the University of Arizona. The Arizona legislature established another narrowly focused commission four years later when it created a 10-member commission to study the feasibility of opening a branch campus of Arizona State University on the west side of Maricopa County.

## Current Conditions

A discussion of state planning methods presupposes that conditions are such that planning is necessary. What are some of the current conditions that institutions, statewide boards, and state governments can anticipate, and which will make it even more imperative in the future for them to consider alternative planning strategies, including blue ribbon commissions?

*First and foremost is the decrease in the numbers of potential students due to an anticipated drop in the birth-rate.* The possibility of fewer students is significant for institutions in the area of funding especially. The amount of funding an institution receives is correlated directly with the number of students enrolled. Fewer students mean less financial support, even though the institution's fixed expenses remain the same. This fact is causing institutions to become exceedingly competitive in the area of adult continuing education and lifelong learning. Some institutions are seeking additional older students through nationwide campaigns. Others are establishing off-campus operations outside the walls of other institutions. These operations, however, raise questions of quality control and consumer protection, and point to an increasing need for regulation and effective state planning.

*A second condition involves fiscal resources.* Inflation and increased costs have been felt by all segments of society. Legislatures and executive offices have responded by increasing the number of specialists on their budget staffs and by reviewing more closely budgets received from insti-

tutions and state boards. No guarantee for the future ensures that higher education will be restored completely to the highly favored position vis-a-vis appropriations it held following World War II. One reason for this is the politicization of faculties and students during the era of the 1960s. Concomitantly, other areas of public service, such as health, energy, and conservation, are claiming more public attention and funding.

*A third condition is the increased demand for greater accountability on the part of institutions and state systems by legislatures and governors' offices.* Accountability no longer is confined to fiscal audit but also encompasses program and performance audits of outcomes, educational results, and effectiveness. More attention also is being given to review of programs. Policy makers are attempting to eliminate duplication of services and programs, and to ensure and protect quality and diversity among institutions.

*The growth of the proprietary sector has added to the problem faced by states.* These institutions are privately owned, usually not accredited, and not under direct control of the education agency in a state, yet their students are eligible to receive state and federal student aid funds.

*The effect of collective bargaining on state planning is another condition that warrants attention.* Richard M. Millard raises several questions as to the future role of collective bargaining.

> *Will it increase or inhibit institutional flexibility in meeting changed conditions? Will it tend to reinforce greater centralization, not necessarily through coordination and planning, but through centralization of the bargaining process? What impact will it have when retrenchment, program review, consolidation, and performance audit come more fully into play?* (Millard 1977, p. 16)

*A sixth condition to consider is the force of federal legislation which usually imposes additional regulations and responsibilities on state agencies and institutions.* A variety of dictates fall beneath this federal umbrella, such as affirmative action and handicapped legislation. Careful delineation of mission, role, and scope, along with effective planning, on the part both of the institution and the state appear to be necessary.

State agencies and state governments wrestle with such conditions. As the charges assigned to blue ribbon commissions reflect efforts to deal with these conditions, it is possible to see some of the reasons for the establishment of such agencies as elements in the planning strategy.

## Summary

State level blue ribbon commissions have been a frequent phenomenon in higher education. Gubernatorially or legislatively created commissions were established on at least 48 occasions in 25 states between 1965 and 1983. In many instances they have made recommendations that have changed the direction of higher education in the state; in other instances their impact has been minimal. The next chapter attempts to identify those factors that enhance a commission's likelihood of success.

# THE ANATOMIES OF TWO STATE-LEVEL COMMISSIONS

The systematic review of state-level blue ribbon commissions discussed in the previous chapter illustrates the ongoing use of these commissions. This chapter will identify characteristics of blue ribbon commissions in two states carefully selected for comparative, in-depth analysis of the conditions that seem related to the relative success or lack of success of such commissions.

The purpose of the study is to discover what elements contribute to the effectiveness or the ineffectiveness of a blue ribbon commission. The decision on which two commissions to select was made carefully with the help of persons in the field of higher education. The ultimate goal in selecting the two states and in constructing the questionnaire was to ensure, as much as possible, that the results generalized from the microcosm of this study could be applied to the macrocosm of blue ribbon commissions in general.

The selection of two particular states and their respective blue ribbon commissions for in-depth analysis was made with the object in mind that a study seeking to discover elements of effectiveness should look at states that appear to have experienced different outcomes from their blue ribbon commissions. Thus, the Temporary State Commission on the Future of Postsecondary Education in New York State (Wessell Commission) and Maryland's Commission on the Structure and Governance of Education (Rosenberg Commission) were selected for discussion here. A major factor in choosing the two commissions was the apparent contrast in the effectiveness of these two commissions. For the purpose of this study, a blue ribbon commission is defined as effective if it appears to have produced an immediate and recognizable change in the postsecondary structure, functions, or processes in a state.

Long-range results emerging from a blue ribbon commission study may not make themselves evident for a long time afterwards. For example, in Alabama recommendations of the Education Study Commission of 1958 dealing with the creation of a statewide coordinating agency were not implemented. However, in 1968 much the same study was made once again by a group called the Alabama Education Study Commission. The findings and recommendations were very much the same, but the recommendations of this commission were acted upon by the legislature and put into effect in 1969. The difference was that over the 10-year period enrollments in higher education and the number of institutions in the state had essentially doubled, so the need for coordination in higher education was much more evident. The first Alabama commission appears to have been ahead of its time and, by definition, was not effective. One could postulate, however, that the commission had a long-term impact.

The Rosenberg Commission report in Maryland was viewed by many as having led to major restructuring of the educational system in that state, whereas the report of the Wessell Commission in New York appeared to have been largely unimplemented. Thus, Rosenberg was effective; Wessell was not.

### Commission Charges and Context

Both commissions were given a broad charge. The legislation, Chapter 346 of the Laws of 1976, which established the New York commission, stated: "It should be the duty of the commission to conduct a comprehensive study of postsecondary education in New York State . . . [and it] shall recommend a detailed plan of action embodying the findings of its studies." The letter of transmittal of the final report of the Wessell Commission to the governor reiterates the same point: "the commission was created out of the belief . . . that the governance and financing of higher education in New York State required serious re-examination and reordering."

The governor's charge to the Maryland commission expressed concern over the increased fiscal commitments of state and local governments in educational expenditures. The letter of transmittal of the final report of the Rosenberg Commission to the governor states that the commission was appointed to study the structure and governance of education in Maryland from early childhood through the graduate school, and among other things to come up with "a proposed structural reform." Both Wessell and Rosenberg were aiming to study the structure, governance, and finance of the statewide educational system.

Both New York and Maryland have had several blue ribbon commissions established during the course of their histories to address a variety of educational concerns. Some commissions in both states may be considered effective in that they produced an immediate and recognizable change in the postsecondary structure, functions, or processes in a state. Their existence indicates that the Wessell and Rosenberg commissions fit into a long series of commissions which handled some of the same problems. It also is interesting to note that the earlier Maryland blue ribbon commissions met with mixed success, while the earlier New York commissions met with overwhelming success (see Tables 6 and 7, pp. 32–36). It should be noted, however, that the New York commissions each basically recommended one specific course of action for a single area of concern, as contrasted with the Maryland experience. Maryland commissions suggested a variety of tasks to achieve the goal set for them. Some were instituted; others were not.

A bird's eye view of the Rosenberg and Wessell commissions—their membership, when they were established, when reports were issued—is provided in Table 8 (p. 37). Membership is especially interesting. The Rosenberg Commission had a large membership, including representatives of many state groups such as minorities and blacks. The Wessell Commission had few members.

### Establishment of the Two Commissions

Maryland and New York, along with the majority of other states, were forced to give consideration to a very different set of circumstances by the middle 1970s than they had faced a decade earlier. Six basic issues demanded attention: rising costs, enrollment decline, the consequences of retrenchment, unemployment, educational quality, and erosion of public trust (Lierheimer 1978, p. 6). Governor Mandel asked the Rosenberg Commission in 1973 to review education in Maryland with regard to the continuing reorganization of state government into departments each headed by its own secretary. In his letter of transmittal, he mentioned the "development of a state cabinet system" and the "escalating financial commitment of state and local governments to public education" as two factors prompting the necessity for the Rosenberg Commission. But "beyond cost factors is the question of whether the system has the inherent capability to respond, in timely fashion, to changing conditions." (Maurer 1976, pp. 21–22). Thus, the Rosenberg commissioners were

*Some commissions . . . produced an immediate and recognizable change in the postsecondary structures, functions, or processes in a state.*

# TABLE 6

## SUMMARY OF MAJOR BLUE RIBBON COMMISSIONS IN EDUCATION IN MARYLAND PRIOR TO THE ROSENBERG COMMISSION

| Year | Commission | Purpose | Recommendations | Effect |
|------|------------|---------|-----------------|--------|
| 1924 | Janney | The University of Maryland was proposing to expand its offerings and to attempt to transform itself from basically an agricultural and mechanical general university curriculum such as was being offered at some of the more renowed state universities in the Midwest. | (1) Maintain the University of Maryland as an agricultural and mechanical arts institution. | (1) in part |
| | | | (2) Establish a "college commission" to coordinate institutions and maintain quality standards. | (2) none |
| | | | (3) Phase out state financial support to independent institutions. | (3) none |
| | | | (4) Revamp the current system of scholarship aid by providing direct aid to students. | (4) none |
| 1931 | Shriver | Increasing numbers of students seeking entrance from high school into higher education institutions. | (1) Further the development of the University of Maryland in light of increases in enrollments. | (1) yes |
| | | | (2) Institute a special student transfer policy if state aid to private institutions was to be continued. | (2) none |
| | | | (3) Convene a study group to look at state-aided institutions with the view to possible redefinition of their role and scope in relation to the overall state needs and to develop a financial program leading to their self-support. | (3) in part |

| Year | Commission | Charge | Recommendations | Status |
|---|---|---|---|---|
| 1937 | Soper | To investigate the comparative offerings of black institutions with white instructions. | (1) State takeover and development of Morgan College. | (1) yes |
| | | | (2) Improve Bowie Normal School and Coppin Normal School (black elementary teacher training institutions). | (2) in part |
| | | | (3) Princess Anne Academy (the eastern branch of the University of Maryland) should be a high school and offer primarily vocational training. | (3) none |
| 1947 | Marbury | To study the issue of access for all who could benefit from higher education and the need to increase in number and quality the programs offered for black students. Emphasis was on the strengthening of the public sector as a means to improve access. | (1) Establish a statewide system of locally controlled, racially integrated, comprehensive two-year colleges. | (1) none |
| | | | (2) Expand University of Maryland to 10,000 enrollment. | (2) none |
| | | | (3) Increase appropriations to Morgan and the development of a graduate school curriculum. | (3) none |
| | | | (4) Establish a permanent state board of higher education. | (4) none |
| | | | (5) Revise student scholarship policy. | (5) none |

## TABLE 6 (continued)

| Year | Commission | Purpose | Recommendations | Effect |
|------|-----------|---------|-----------------|--------|
| 1955 | Pullen | To explore ways to accommodate a dramatically increased student population. | (1) Establish community college system.<br>(2) Urge all liberal arts institutions to bolster existing programs rather than undertaking rapid expansion.<br>(3) Institutions should develop and utilize quantifiable admissions data to funnel students into appropriate institutions suited to their academic level.<br>(4) Expand teacher education programs and professional schools and establish programs for librarians and social workers.<br>(5) Encourage more Maryland youth to go into higher education through coordinated counseling programs and preferential admissions policies for residents.<br>(6) Increase funding to state institutions.<br>(7) Initiate a system of direct state scholarships.<br>(8) Establish a permanent state advisory commission on higher education. | (1) yes<br>(2) yes<br><br>(3) none<br><br><br>(4) in part<br><br><br>(5) yes<br><br><br>(6) yes<br>(7) none<br><br>(8) none |
| 1960 | Warfield | To explore ways to accommodate more increases in enrollments. Discussion was centered around access and quality issues and how the University of Maryland could meet state needs. | (1) Expand University of Maryland.<br>(2) Amalgamate three teachers colleges into the university. | (1) none<br>(2) in part |

| 1962 | Curlett | To consider how to reorganize the state educational system and thereby meet state needs. | (1) Establish a tripartite system whereby the state teachers colleges would enlarge their scope and mission to include general liberal arts curricula in addition to teacher training and thus become a state college system. The other two elements of the tripartite group were to be the existing community colleges and the University of Maryland. | (1) yes |
|---|---|---|---|---|
| | | | (2) Institute a single board of trustees for Morgan State College and the state teachers colleges. | (2) no |
| | | | (3) Create a division of higher education within the state Department of Education with responsibility for the community colleges. | (3) yes |
| | | | (4) Maintain the board of regents of the University of Maryland. | (4) yes |
| | | | (5) Create an Advisory Council for Higher Education. | (5) yes |

## TABLE 7

### SUMMARY OF MAJOR BLUE RIBBON COMMISSIONS IN EDUCATION IN NEW YORK STATE PRIOR TO THE WESSELL COMMISSION

| Year | Commission | Purpose | Recommendations | Effect |
|------|------------|---------|-----------------|--------|
| 1948 | Young | To explore ways to accommodate increased enrollments and to promote access. | To remove the 11 state teachers colleges from under the purview of the board of regents, and give these colleges their own board of trustees to be appointed by the governor. | yes |
| 1959 | Heald | To meet the increasing demand for higher education in New York State. | To expand the state university and community college system. | yes |
| 1967 | Bundy | To preserve the strength and vitality of the private and independent institutions of higher education, yet at the same time keep them free. | To establish a scale of financial support to private or independent institutions based on the number and level of degrees conferred. | yes |
| 1972 | Keppel | To look at higher education finance. | To establish the Tuition Assistance Program (TAP) which is a need-based entitlement program with awards limited to the size of tuition. | yes |

# TABLE 8

## GENERAL COMPARISON OF DATA CONCERNING THE WESSELL AND ROSENBERG COMMISSIONS

| Wessell Commission | Rosenberg Commission |
|---|---|
| *Purpose:* To re-examine and reorder the governance and financing of higher education in New York State including the impact of the New York City fiscal crisis upon the City University. | *Purpose:* To study the organization of Maryland's educational enterprise. |
| *Membership:* five commissioners including a student, university president, lawyer, foundation president, and vice president of the College Entrance Examination Board. | *Membership:* 27 commissioners including representatives of business, government, citizens, blacks, women, and former educators. |
| *Appointment:* Members appointed by Governor Hugh L. Carey in August 1976. | *Appointment:* Members appointed by Governor Maxium Mandel in January 1973. |
| *Final Report:* Issued in March 1977. | *Final Report:* Issued in May 1975. |

*. . . asked to take a "fresh look" at the structure and governance of the entire spectrum of education and to make "workable" recommendations for change* (Maurer 1976, p. 21).

This forward-looking orientation of the Rosenberg Commission was not to be found in the reasons for the establishment of the Wessell Commission. The major impetus for its establishment was fiscal crisis.

The City University of New York (CUNY) has been a tradition in New York City since 1847. It was the third largest university system in the nation, had always offered free tuition and, since 1969, had an open-admissions policy to any graduate of a New York City high school. The City of New York traditionally had been CUNY's main funding agent. But 1975 was a particularly drastic year financially for New York City. On the brink of default, the city cut back $32 million from the CUNY budget which, when a variety of matching funds was taken into account, actually amounted to $64 million.

In the spring of 1976, New York City announced that its half share of funding the four CUNY senior colleges would cease in 1977–78 and that New York State would have to fill the breach. It was at this junction that Governor Carey appointed the Wessell Commission. The charge to the commission was broad and included a comprehensive study of postsecondary education in New York State, the role of the board of regents, the relationship of CUNY to the state, the city, and to other institutions involving the private sector, and the financing of CUNY.

**Rosenberg Commission: Recommendations and Outcome**
The Rosenberg Commission proposed the following system for education in Maryland. There would be two boards, a State Board for Elementary and Secondary Education and a State Board for Higher Education. Each would have 15 lay members appointed by the governor for six-year staggered terms, including a member from each congressional district. Each board would be responsible for selecting its own chair and its own commissioner—the latter being a professional educator (Rosenberg 1975, p. 20).

The two boards would meet together a minimum of four times annually as the Joint Education Board and would select three candidates for the position of Chairman of the Joint Education Board. No candidate was to be a member of either board, and final selection of this chairman would rest with the governor. A salaried and a full-time employee, the chairman would serve as the governor's cabinet member for education, preside over meetings of the Joint Education Board, achieving inter-board coordination, and present and defend the budgets of the two state boards to the governor.

The Joint Education Board should coordinate the two separate boards. The Rosenberg Commission proposed a series of councils to be established by, and to report to, the Joint Education Board. These were to be composed of both board and nonboard members and were to "assist the educational structure in coping with the complexities of the future" (Rosenberg 1975, p. 22). The councils would have at least three functions:

*(1) To serve as a unit of educational governmental apparatus to plan, organize, and monitor services which do not clearly fall within the separate purviews of elementary and secondary or postsecondary education;*

*(2) To provide a stance of advocacy for students who have special needs and requirements that tend to be disregarded by the ongoing system;*

*(3) To advocate reform and new procedures.* (Rosenberg 1975, p. 22).

Councils were to have their own staffs, but were not envisioned as permanent bodies. Seven such councils were recommended, although no limit was placed on the number at any one time.

The restructuring of postsecondary education proposed by the Rosenberg Commission elicited concern from the affected parties. In the wake of public response to the commission report, the governor appointed a task force to review the recommendations.

The Wilner Task Force had 11 members: seven had served as members on the Rosenberg Commission; three were state senators and three were delegates serving in the Maryland House. The chair was Judge Alan M. Wilner of the Maryland Court of Special Appeals.

Most people agreed that the commission had identified a number of problems that needed addressing, and that some of its recommendations were conceptually sound. Wilner said that the problem was in the specific solutions that were suggested.

> *Our function was not to redo the work of the Rosenberg Commission, but rather to find a way to recast the basic recommendations of that commission so as to make them workable if adopted and palatable to the legislature.**

In other words, the Rosenberg Commission suggested and induced changes in the postsecondary system in Maryland, while the Wilner Task Force operated as a vehicle set up to mediate between proposed change and entrenched interests. A person who served on both the commission and the task force and was also a member of the House of Delegates commented that the legislative task force "greased the skids" for passage of change-producing legislation.

The Wilner Task Force held five public hearings in various locations, plus three invitational hearings at which representatives from the various educational institutions and agencies of the state and local governments presented their reactions to the study commission's recommendations, as well as their own alternative proposals. Various individuals, groups, and agencies submitted letters and position papers. The task force addressed all and amended some of the recommendations of the Rosenberg Commission.

As a result, Senate Bill 347, enacted by the Maryland General Assembly during the 1976 regular session, implemented the Wilner Task Force recommendations. The Rosenberg Commission can be said to have been effective since it produced immediate and recognizable change in the postsecondary education structure, function, or processes in the state.

**Wessell Commission: Recommendations and Outcome**
The Wessell Commission put forth five major recommendations. They dealt with the need for immediate assistance

*(Wilner 1980, letter.)

to the senior colleges of CUNY; suggested restructuring the State University of New York (SUNY) and CUNY "to preserve and enhance the quality, specific missions, and traditions of access characteristic of public higher education in New York"; the enhancement of student access and opportunities; the maintenance and enhancement of the contributions of the private sector; the strengthening of the policy-making and planning functions of the state board of regents, "provided their effectiveness is improved by a new appointment procedure"; (Wessell 1977, pp. 24–25).

Financial assistance to CUNY commenced in the 1980–81 fiscal year, almost three years after the issuance of the final report of the Wessell Commission. The implemented plan began with a similar concept to the Wessell recommendation but extended and modified it over a three-year period to end in an ultimate state takeover of CUNY. The suggested restructuring of SUNY and CUNY was rejected in all its parts by the New York State Legislature. The Legislature took positive action on one of nine sections of the Wessell Commission recommendations regarding student access and opportunities by approving in 1978 the $300 increase in the award ceiling of the Tuition Assistance Program (TAP).

The commission also had recommended the elimination of the $100 minimum TAP award. The Legislature, however, decided to double the amount. One section of three on the commission recommendation concerning the private sector received legislative action. This section referred to the Bundy aid program.* In the 1977 and 1979 sessions, the Legislature voted to increase the Bundy aid amount. The Legislature rejected all parts of the recommendation suggesting changes in the responsibilities and appointment procedures of the state board of regents. Obviously, the Wessell Commission cannot be considered effective on the basis of the outcome of its recommendations.

*The Wessell Commission cannot be considered effective on the basis of the outcome of its recommendations.*

### Determining Elements Relating to Commission Effectiveness
In order to discover what particular elements of a blue ribbon commission seem to be related to its ultimate effec-

---

*Section 6401 of the Education Law (1968) brought into effect "Bundy Aid" which is a scale of financial support to private or independent institutions based on the level and number of degrees conferred.

---

## TABLE 9
### FAVORABLE RESPONSES TO QUESTIONS
### ABOUT THE COMMISSION

| Questions | Rosenberg | | Wessell | |
|---|---|---|---|---|
| | Number | Percent | Number | Percent |
| Using a blue ribbon commission was appropriate to address the issues. | 20 | 95.24 | 21 | 84.00 |
| The objectives of the commission were clear and precise. | 9 | 60.00 | 11 | 57.89 |
| The objectives of the commission seemed attainable. | 8 | 80.00 | 4 | 28.57 |
| Adequate time was allocated for the commission to complete its report. | 21 | 95.45 | 6 | 21.43 |
| The commission experienced at least some delay in getting underway. | 14 | 87.50 | 19 | 82.61 |
| The commission had sufficient funds. | 16 | 100.00 | 16 | 88.89 |

tiveness a variety of persons in both New York and Maryland who had knowledge of, or involvement with, either of the commissions were surveyed. This included commission members and staff, legislators, gubernatorial and legislative staff, state higher education executive officers and staff, state board members, consultants to the commission, media persons, scholars, public and private college presidents, university system administrators, and foundation executives [see Johnson 1982].

### Commission
The opinions of all Rosenberg and Wessell respondents on questions relating to their respective commissions in general are presented in Table 9.

Even with the complexities before both states in terms of the reasons for setting up some kind of study group to face new conditions as described above, it is apparent from responses received that most of the people involved favored using the commission approach.

The type of decisions that each state had to make were not only difficult ones, but also potentially unpopular, at least for some of the parties that would be adversely affected from their own particular standpoint. Another type of agency or structure, such as a task force or a legislative subcommittee study, could have been used instead of the blue ribbon commission, but it appears that using a special commission of this type was regarded by a variety of publics as being a valid and appropriate planning strategy.

It is interesting to note that this opinion was held by representatives of the ineffective commission as well as the effective one. As basic as this may sound, it is important for people who may serve on a commission, or may consider establishing one, to know that a blue ribbon commission represents a respectable and potentially successful alternative problem-solving mechanism.

Once a blue ribbon commission has been established, it is presented with a formal charge or set of objectives. A commission may establish its own specific objectives reflecting the more general statements conveyed by the formal charge. Both Rosenberg and Wessell respondents described their respective commission's objectives as clear and precise.

A striking difference between the two commissions surfaced when it came to opinions concerning the second part of the question about objectives. This had to do with their perceived attainability. Overwhelmingly, the effective Rosenberg Commission respondents claimed that their set of objectives was attainable, while the ineffective commission respondents saw their set of objectives as unattainable. One could argue this is due to the "halo" effect. All Rosenberg respondents spoke favorably about the commission and its accomplishments. Since its recommendations were attained in the end, it is possible that, in looking back, people's responses reflected the satisfactory outcome of the commission.

However, considering the range of respondents in terms of their relationships to the two commissions, that does not satisfactorily account for the dichotomy of opinion. Instead, it appears that for any commission to be successful, it is very important that the goals and objectives set for the commission are believed to be achievable.

Another apparently crucial factor for success is allowing a sufficient amount of time for the commission to do its work. Here again, the dichotomy of responses was blatant. As noted earlier, the Rosenberg Commission study lasted for almost two and one–half years, while the Wessell Commission was given approximately nine months to complete its study. Responses indicate a definite need to have a realistic or sufficient amount of time allotted for the commission to operate effectively. Obviously, the amount of time necessary for any particular commission to complete its study is dependent upon the breadth of the charge and the intricacies of the issues under study. It would be foolhardy to try to specify exactly how long a hypothetical commission with hypothetical objectives might require.

A blue ribbon commission can experience some delay in beginning operations. Getting acquainted, getting organized, and getting staffed and started sometimes can take longer than anticipated. Experiencing some initial delay before beginning operations does not have an effect on the success of the ultimate work of the commission. Naturally, this presupposes that the initial delay is not interminable and that there is still a reasonable amount of time to conduct the study.

The final question in the group of questions relating to the topic area of the commission in general had to do with funding. Responses indicate that respondents of both commissions believed the commission was given sufficient funds to accomplish successfully its objectives. Therefore, the presence of enough money does not ensure ultimate success. This does not imply that a dearth of funding will not have an adverse impact on a commission. Rather, the availability of sufficient funds is not perceived as having an effect on the outcomes of the study.

### Commissioners

Opinions of all Rosenberg and Wessell respondents to questions relating to characteristics of the commissioners is presented in Table 10. These questions probed topics such as commissioner selection, suitability, and dedication.

For both commissions the selection of the commissioners was to take into account major affected interests (e.g., sectors, university systems). Several respondents of the Rosenberg commission declared that the emphasis in com-

TABLE 10

## FAVORABLE RESPONSES TO
## QUESTIONS ABOUT THE COMMISSIONERS

| Questions | Rosenberg | | Wessell | |
|---|---|---|---|---|
| | Number | Percent | Number | Percent |
| The selection of commissioners took into account the major affected interests. | 15 | 75.00 | 18 | 69.23 |
| The commissioners were well suited to perform their required functions. | 15 | 78.95 | 13 | 56.52 |
| The commissioners gave great attention to the commission's activities. | 13 | 76.47 | 2 | 11.76 |
| The commissioners met enough times. | 14 | 100.00 | 8 | 47.06 |
| The commissioners were accessible to persons wishing to comment. | 18 | 94.74 | 12 | 60.00 |
| The chairman provided good to excellent leadership to the commission. | 12 | 66.67 | 10 | 47.62 |

missioner selection had been on getting well-qualified, "blue ribbon" citizenry. It is significant to note that the Rosenberg Commission included key legislators among its members. The inclusion of legislators can be especially important during the implementation process when often one of the commission objectives is to pass appropriate legislation. By being a part of the commission throughout its deliberations, legislators usually can offer a unique perspective on the issues and will be thoroughly conversant with the study when it comes before the full legislature.

Commissioners serving on both the effective and the ineffective commissions were perceived by a majority of respondents as well suited to handle the issues. However, a minority of persons thought that the ineffective commission members were poorly suited and made some comments to this effect.

A large majority of Rosenberg commissioners were perceived as giving a great amount of attention to the activities of the commission. This is in striking contrast to the Wessell commissioners who were perceived by only a small minority of respondents as giving commission activities great attention. However, the large majority (71 percent) of respondents described the Wessell commissioners as giving a moderate amount of attention to the activities (all respondents for the Rosenberg Commission perceived that the commissioners gave at least moderate attention to the activities). The trend and tendency that is exhibited by these data are sufficient to suggest that the more attention the commissioners personally can give to the commission activities, the more likely it is to be successful.

The question concerning the perceived quality of the leadership of the chairman of the commission produced some mixed responses. By and large, the successful commission was seen by the majority as having had very good leadership; opinions on the unsuccessful one were fairly well split down the middle between good and fair/poor. The differences were not significant statistically. However, more of the Rosenberg responses indicated excellent leadership, and none indicated poor leadership (although a number of Wessell respondents thought that leadership was poor).

One factor that was found to discriminate strongly between the successful and unsuccessful commission was whether the commissioners believed they had met together enough times. The definition of "enough times" in terms of an actual number is not practical here since it necessarily will change depending upon any number of variables particular to specific commissions. Nonetheless, there is a definite relationship between the number of times the commissioners met and the successful commission.

An equally great distinction was apparent between the successful and unsuccessful commission in terms of the accessibility of the commissioners to persons who may wish to talk with them or make comments to them about the issues under deliberation.

### Staff

The opinion of all Rosenberg and Wessell respondents to questions relating to the staff which supported the commission is presented in Table 11. The Rosenberg Commission was aided by a professional staff of eight, while the Wessell Commission had a staff of 12 professionals. However, the Rosenberg Commission had a two-year time frame plus

## TABLE 11

## FAVORABLE RESPONSES TO
## QUESTIONS ABOUT THE STAFF

| Questions | Rosenberg | | Wessell | |
|---|---|---|---|---|
| | Number | Percent | Number | Percent |
| The number of staff was sufficient. | 14 | 100.00 | 12 | 52.17 |
| The staff was chosen on basis of merit alone. | 13 | 81.25 | 6 | 33.33 |
| The skills, background, and experience of the staff was excellent or good. | 13 | 86.67 | 16 | 84.21 |
| There was great to moderate depth and breath to the background research conducted by the staff. | 14 | 87.50 | 13 | 54.17 |
| For the duration of the study, relevant research was conducted by the staff at least intermittently. | 13 | 86.67 | 18 | 94.74 |
| The staff was often or always accessible to persons wishing to comment. | 15 | 93.75 | 20 | 90.91 |

an extension in which to complete work whereas the Wessell Commission had a six-month time frame.

This staff variable was another one which strongly discriminated between the successful and unsuccessful commission, with the successful commission respondents agreeing that the number of staff assigned to the commission was sufficient to complete the assignment in the time allotted.

Another highly significant difference between the two commissions can be discovered in examining perceptions about how the staff was chosen. Many more persons affiliated with the effective commission thought that the staff had been selected solely on the basis of merit. More than half of the respondents of the ineffective commission believed that political relationships and other (unspecified) factors also had played a part in staff selection. Nonetheless, both groups rated the skills, background, and experience as good to excellent. This was also the case with respect to the amount of relevant research (surveys, data gathering, etc.) conducted by the staff during the study. However, there was a dichotomy of opinion with regard to the depth and breadth of the background research conducted by the staff. Wessell Commission respondents were significantly less positive about staff than were the Rosenberg respondents. Interestingly, when a statistical comparison of responses is made between this question and the question concerning the basis for staff selection, those respondents who perceived that the staff was selected on the basis of merit alone also perceived that the depth and breadth of the background research conducted by the staff was moderate to great. Conversely those respondents perceiving that the staff was not selected on the basis of merit were less positive about the depth and breadth of the background research of the staff (Johnson 1982).

Apparently staff members for both commissions maintained an open stance regarding people who wished to come forward and offer their comments. Earlier it was noted that this was not always the case with the commissioners of the ineffective commission.

### External Elements

Responses to questions concerning external elements affecting the commission are given in Table 12.

Both commissions held public hearings and a majority of respondents from both judged that they had held them at about the right frequency. Public hearings are a useful vehicle for increasing public awareness of the commission and its work. They also provide an important forum for the voicing of concerns by the various potentially affected publics. Of course, the appropriate number of public hearings will vary from commission to commission.

The perceived utilization of testimony from public hearings, however, is very important. Rosenberg respondents perceived such testimony as carrying equal weight along with other research in the deliberations of the commission. More than half of the Wessell respondents reported that public hearing testimony was either ignored completely or considered only when politically necessary (Johnson 1982).

## TABLE 12
### FAVORABLE RESPONSES TO
### QUESTIONS ABOUT THE EXTERNAL ELEMENTS

| Questions | Rosenberg | | Wessell | |
|---|---|---|---|---|
| | Number | Percent | Number | Percent |
| Public hearings were held just about in the right frequency. | 18 | 90.00 | 15 | 72.22 |
| Testimony from public hearings was relied upon, or considered with other research. | 17 | 85.00 | 8 | 42.11 |
| The commission sought media coverage. | 12 | 75.00 | 13 | 54.17 |
| Reaction in the media to the commission was favorable. | 14 | 93.33 | 2 | 13.33 |
| There was repeated use of experts other than commission members and staff. | 14 | 82.35 | 8 | 47.06 |
| Involvement of the governor was mild to avid. | 10 | 55.56 | 15 | 83.33 |

The effective commission respondents indicated that media coverage had been sought and also that media reaction had been positive. The ineffective commission respondents, however, were divided in their opinion on the extent to which media coverage was sought, but overwhelmingly reported that media reaction was unfavorable.

Another important difference between the two commissions was in the repeated use of experts. Successful commission respondents differed from their unsuccessful counterparts in reporting more frequently that experts (other than commission members and staff) had been used repeatedly. This repeated use of experts is important because a broad base of input into a commission's deliberative process adds immeasurably to a sense of fair play and earnest investigation on the part of participants, observers, and affected parties.

Both respondent groups largely perceived the involvement of the governor in the work of the commission as being mild (respectively 50 percent and 67 percent of the Rosenberg and Wessell respondents reported mild involvement). However, judging by additional comments and interviews, the mild involvement was viewed in a positive light by the effective group and in a negative light by the ineffective group. The perception of why the respective governors established the commission differed. In the case of the successful commission, the motivation was construed as being to better an existing condition. By contrast, the motivation behind establishing the other commission was perceived as being to ameliorate a crisis.

Therefore, the mild involvement of the governor was perceived by one group as illustrating a sense of confidence and benign neglect in the commission and its work, whereas the other group perceived the mild involvement as illustrating an escapist tactic and further proof that the governor wanted to deflect criticisms from himself. Obviously, the public clarification of purpose, importance, and potential by the governor with respect to a commission could do much to set a positive scene for the commission's work and its subsequent acceptance.

### Commission Output

Percentage responses to questions concerning the final report, its recommendations, and implementation appear in Table 13. Both groups felt that the final recommendations addressed the commission's objectives as outlined by the respective governor. However, the final reports differed between the successful and the unsuccessful commission in that the latter did not present enough of a rationale to buttress the specific recommendations. In other words, it is very important that the final report does not merely list the recommendations, but elaborates and explains the reasons for and implications of each.

Another interesting note is that the final report of the effective commission called for radical changes. However, subsequent to the issuing of this report and the furor it created, the governor appointed a task force composed of legislators and educators to work closely with the various sectors, listen to a few public hearings, and develop palatable and workable compromise objectives.

In the face of the likely wholesale rejection of controversial recommendations of future commissions, a subsidiary,

TABLE 13
**FAVORABLE RESPONSES TO**
**QUESTIONS ABOUT THE COMMISSION OUTPUT**

| Questions | Rosenberg | | Wessell | |
|---|---|---|---|---|
| | Number | Percent | Number | Percent |
| The final recommendations addressed all or some of the objectives. | 19 | 95.00 | 21 | 84.00 |
| The final report of the commission amply substantiated the recommendations. | 12 | 63.16 | 6 | 25.00 |
| The political potency of major affected interests was, at least somewhat, considered by the commission in its efforts towards implementation of the final recommendations. | 17 | 85.00 | 12 | 44.44 |
| The majority of the commissioners were at least generally active in seeking implementation of the final recommendations. | 9 | 50.00 | 3 | 13.04 |
| The commission report led to changes in policies and procedures by other than legislators. | 18 | 81.82 | 5 | 19.23 |

short-term task force can be an effective strategy to mediate between the ideal and the real and, thus, arrive at least to some degree at change in a reasonable direction.

An earlier question asked if the selection of the commissioners had taken into account the major affected interests (e.g. sectors, university systems). There was no significant difference between the two commissions in that the majority of both groups believed that in fact they had done so.

However, a striking contrast of opinion becomes apparent when the question is directed toward the implementation process, and revised to discover if the political potency of the major affected interests was considered by the commission in attempting to implement the final recommendations. The effective commission was positive that this had been done to a great extent; the ineffective commission respondents held much more negative views.

Future commissions ought to pay careful attention during the implementation process to those groups or institutions that will have to respond to the recommendations. Misunderstandings and mutinies can impede or halt the proposed changes. It is also very important that the majority of commissioners play an active role in seeking implementation of the final recommendations. Commissioners should view their work as ongoing past the completion of the final report. Their presence and work during implementation lends credibility to the work and recommendations of the commission and appears to contribute to the ultimate effectiveness of a commission.

Finally, the effective commission placed more reliance than did the ineffective one upon changes in policies and procedures to be implemented by individuals or groups other than legislators. Change through legislation is often the goal of a blue ribbon commission but it does not have to be the sole aim. Much useful change can be effected without the force of law. A commission should keep an open view to making other suggestions or providing alternative courses of action that can be pursued. This has the added advantage of providing a flexible and potentially less threatening avenue for change that can be tailored by the affected parties.

### Subsequent Effect

The subsequent effects on postsecondary education perceived by the respondents from the two commissions is addressed in Table 14, dealing with change in postsecondary education structure or process and the influence of the commission.

One question concerned the degree that subsequent change in postsecondary education was due to the work and recommendations of the commission, and is pivotal. If an effective commission is defined as one where its work and recommendations produce change, then the majority of the Rosenberg respondents perceived their commission as effective. Conversely, the majority of the Wessell respondents perceived their commission as ineffective.

Rosenberg and Wessell respondents disagree with regard to the degree that subsequent change in postsecondary education was due to the work and recommendations of the respective commissions. The Rosenberg respondents, with only four exceptions out of 23, reported that the degree of subsequent change was some/great. By contrast,

## TABLE 14
### FAVORABLE RESPONSES TO QUESTIONS ABOUT THE SUBSEQUENT EFFECT OF THE COMMISSION

| Questions | Rosenberg | | Wessell | |
|---|---|---|---|---|
| | Number | Percent | Number | Percent |
| Subsequent change in postsecondary education was due to the work and recommendations of the commission. | 19 | 82.61 | 3 | 11.11 |
| At least some similar changes would have come about without the commission being called into being. | 18 | 81.82 | 18 | 81.82 |
| The influence of the commission was constructive. | 19 | 82.61 | 7 | 28.00 |

the Wessell respondents, with only four exceptions out of 28, reported that the degree of subsequent change was minor/none. The majority of Rosenberg and Wessell respondents indicated that similar changes would have come about even if the commission had not been called into being. However, it is important to note that the heaviest concentration of Rosenberg respondents qualified their answer by selecting the descriptor "some"; the bulk of the Wessell respondents selected the outright "yes," denoting that unqualifiably similar changes would have come about without the commission.

With reference to the influence of the commission on postsecondary education, the two groups again disagree in their respective responses. The Rosenberg respondents concentrated at the positive end of the possible responses and reported that the influence of the commission on postsecondary education had been constructive. The majority of Wessell respondents reported that the commission had no influence on postsecondary education.

### Synopsis
Some conditions and characteristics associated with blue ribbon commissions were explored through the survey described in this chapter. Certain characteristics appear to contribute to the ultimate effectiveness of a blue ribbon

commission. Translating these positive characteristics into specific suggestions, the most outstanding are as follows:

1. *The goals and objectives set for the commission should be attainable.*
2. *The commission should be given a sufficient amount of time to accomplish its goals and complete its report.*
3. *The commissioners should meet together enough times.*
4. *The commissioners should be accessible to persons wishing to comment.*
5. *The commission should be assigned a sufficient number of staff to complete the assignment in the time allocated.*
6. *The staff of the commission should be chosen on the basis of merit.*
7. *The commission should make use of the testimony it receives from public hearings.*
8. *The commission should make use of experts other than commission members and staff.*
9. *The final report of the commission should explain the reasons for and implications of each recommendation.*
10. *The political potency of the major affected interests (e.g., sectors) should be considered by the commission in its efforts toward implementation of final recommendations.*
11. *The commissioners should play an active role in seeking implementation of the final recommendations.*

# BLUE RIBBON COMMISSIONS ON CAMPUS

Generally, the blue ribbon commission approach has been reserved for the national and state levels. Colleges and universities, when attempting to resolve important issues, traditionally have relied upon the wisdom of standing committees or specially appointed task forces composed of members of the campus community. In most cases this approach has produced satisfactory results. However, there may be times when a different model may be more useful. One common example is the use of external consultants to assist an academic department in assessing the quality of its curriculum and scholarly activity. While the department's own faculty may (and should) prepare a comprehensive self-study, objectivity requires that this effort be reviewed by a disinterested person with unassailable credentials in the particular field (Marcus, Leone, and Goldberg 1983, pp. 41–43).

Other occasions where outside assistance is helpful and where a blue ribbon panel can contribute include when campuses are deeply divided over a specific issue. A fresh view may be required to resolve the problem in a manner that will settle the immediate question and reduce (or eliminate) the level of rancor so that the campus might be pulled back together. Another situation which calls for an outside panel of experts occurs when a college or university seeks to develop ties with, or expand its services to, a particular sector outside of the institution. For example, if a business program wants to enhance its activity with the business community, the advice of a panel of leaders from business and industry is likely to result in a plan which would be attractive to the business sector and, thus, provide greater opportunity for internships, contract research projects, and corporate giving. A third situation when a blue ribbon commission might be appropriate is when a college or university seeks to establish for itself a planning agenda intended to move it to a position of leadership in the region, or among institutions of similar size and mission. In such an instance, the institution needs to be sure that its new direction is in line with broader societal concerns. Who better to involve in such a venture than acknowledged leaders of that society?

While it is difficult to ascertain the frequency to which colleges and universities have resorted to the blue ribbon commission approach, some examples illustrate the point.

*A blue ribbon panel can contribute . . . when campuses are deeply divided over a specific issue.*

### A Campus Divided

A New Jersey college found itself to be in an impossible situation in the spring of 1982. After conducting a national search for a new director of the library, a faculty-staff search committee narrowed the pool of candidates. Among the final group was a white female, the library director at a smaller institution who also had a part-time affiliation with a major university library (the result of an earlier one-year visiting appointment at the university). This candidate, who had a master's degree, had the best interview and the strongest references. In second place was a black male with a doctorate who had held an important position in a major research university library and was director of a library in a nonresearch public university until he had a falling out with the president over funding for the library. On paper, he was the stronger of the two candidates but his interview on campus was not as positive as that of the successful candidate.

This particular college was a leader in the state in the area of faculty affirmative action. However, progress was not as great in the upper administration. One white female dean, one black male director, and one Hispanic male dean (the first in academic affairs, the latter two in student affairs) were at the level in question. The appointment of either candidate would have promoted the college's affirmative action goals. Based on the advice of the search committee, the president offered the position to the woman who promptly accepted. She gave notice to her current employer, put her house on the market, and sought a new home near the college.

When the personnel resolution came to the board of trustees for approval, what was usually a routine action became a major controversy. An unnamed staff member confidentially had informed a trustee that the search was flawed and that racism had been a factor in the decision. When the board member made this known at the meeting, the rest of the board declined to act on the president's nomination. The board member demanded an investigation of the matter by the state's public advocate or by an administrative law judge, but the full board accorded the president the opportunity to conduct the review.

The president's inquiry began with the college's affirmative action officer who had certified the search earlier but was now stating that he had done so under duress. His reservations concerned his interpretation of the language contained in several interview report forms filed by search committee members, as well as his understanding of the discussion that the academic vice president had with the committee prior to its final decision. (The vice president, knowing that the recommendation was likely to generate controversy, had asked the committee to be certain of its decision.) The affirmative action officer had earlier raised his concern with the president who told the affirmative action officer to do what he thought was right, but to do it quickly. The affirmative action officer took this to be pressure to sign the certification form and did so.

When the board next met, the president reported that his investigation revealed no reason to change his recommendation. However, the board member, who earlier raised the issue, claimed to have documented evidence of racism in the search and the board, in closed session, declined to make an appointment. At the board's open session, the faculty attempted to discuss the matter with the board, but the meeting degenerated into a shouting match between the faculty leadership and the board chair.

Several months into the fray, there was no resolution of the matter, the campus was racially divided, most faculty had lined up behind the president in the fight with the board, and the newly appointed acting academic vice president, along with four of the five divisional chairs (a few months earlier called academic deans), informed the president of their intention to resign their administrative posts and return to the faculty in protest. The overwhelming majority of the chairs of the academic programs stated their intention to resign if the matter were not resolved. The community turned to the state's chancellor of higher education who appointed a blue ribbon committee to study the situation.

The committee had three members. Its chair was a former member of the U.S. Civil Rights Commission. The other members were law professors, one from Howard University, the other from Temple University. The group included a white female, a black male, and a white male. The chancellor asked the panel to:

*(1) Review the college's policies and procedures regarding the filling of vacancies; (2) review the college's poli-*

*cies, procedures, and plans regarding affirmative action;*
*(3) review the procedures established for this search*
*. . . ; (4) review the process as it actually occurred in*
*this instance; and (5) make a report and recommenda-*
*tions to the board of trustees and to the chancellor*
(Fleming 1982, p. 2).

He provided the group with a member of his own staff to
furnish administrative support. Having been given exten-
sive background material, the committee spent the better
part of a week on campus. It had complete access to the
files and to the personnel of the college. It scheduled interviews with persons involved with the search, and met with
any person or group requesting to speak to the committee.

Its report addressed the matters at hand—the college's
affirmative action policies and plans, the problem of conflict when either of two affirmative action goals can be met
in one search, and the appointment of a librarian. But, the
group went on to comment about a fundamental problem at
the college—the lack of communication between the board
and the college community—which has "weakened the
educational community." A discussion would clear up
some points that appear to be "dividing the groups and
would definitely ease some of the tensions that now exist"
(Fleming 1982, p. 6). The panel pointed out that external
experts

*cannot relieve an educational community of the respon-*
*sibility of using its own opportunities for communication*
*in order to come to grips with the fundamental issues*
*that are presented to it by a specific case* (Fleming 1982,
p. 6).

The college's board followed the advice. It used the
committee's review of the facts as the basis for conversa-
tion with the college community. As a result, it agreed to
offer the position to the person originally nominated by the
president, and to put into place a number of specific recommendations made by the blue ribbon panel.

**Resolving Problems Prior to Impasse**
Colleges and universities need not wait until a problem
reaches impasse prior to calling together special commit-

tees. A variation of this concept was used in 1978 when a President's Assembly on State Policy Research at the University of Illinois was convened "to explore a series of questions related to interactions between universities and the agencies which create public policy" (Gove and Zollinger 1979, p. iii). In order to initiate a resolution to the "suspicions and reservations" between university faculty and state government concerning public policy research, a three-day meeting was held between faculty and officials representing the legislature, governor, and various state agencies. Among the assembled were some faculty from other institutions and a California assemblyman. Papers and speeches were presented by 14 persons, seven were University of Illinois faculty (p. 121).

As a result, the assembly recommended the strengthening of public policy research "through the utilization and possible expansion of existing linkages between the university and state government." Encouraging closer relations between faculty and government, the assembly suggested that the university conduct symposia on topics relating to policy research and that it involve state government officials in their planning. However, it cautioned against any arrangements "that would adversely affect the academic independence of the university" (Gove and Zollinger 1979, pp. 3–4).

## Planning in Multicampus Institutions

Blue ribbon commissions also have been utilized to make recommendations concerning planning and coordination in multicampus settings. For example, a Joint Committee on Higher Education Planning was established by the chair of both the board of trustees of the University of Vermont and the Vermont State Colleges in order to recommend an appropriate organizational scheme to provide better coordination and planning of Vermont's higher education programs (Smallwood 1971). In 1975, Wisconsin Governor Patrick Lucey asked the University of Wisconsin board of regents to develop a plan to phase out, reduce, or consolidate institutions and programs in the system, and to draft language authorizing such a program as part of the 1975–1977 biennial budget. A blue ribbon panel assisted in this effort. Similarly, when the state university system in Florida sought to assess the need and to develop a plan for educational outreach programs in the state, it created a 29-member Commission on Educational Outreach and Service (Crosby 1976). Major planning efforts of a comprehensive nature also were undertaken by outsiders at the University of Massachusetts and the University of Maryland.

## Setting Future Directions

### An Agenda for the Seventies

The President's Committee on the Future University of Massachusetts was commissioned in 1970 by the newly installed president, Robert C. Wood (Alden 1971, p. i). Headed by Vernon R. Alden, chair of the board of the Boston Company, the committee included four other corporate leaders, a newspaper publisher, two editors, two foundation representatives, a labor leader, a social services administrator, seven educators (including three faculty from the university), and two students.

Citing the unprecedented growth period of the preceding decade, Wood asked the committee to consider:

- *What principal forces in terms of population pressures, economic growth, technological changes, and manpower requirements will play upon the university, and what responsibilities will it consequently be asked to assume?*
- *What changes can and should we anticipate in the university as a community in its style of living and in the working relationships among faculty, students, administration, and alumni?*
- *What changes are necessary and desirable in the content of what the university learns through research and teaches through instruction; and how do we balance the reliable acquisition of knowledge with its humane use?*
- *How should the total educational responsibility of the state be shared among public and private institutions; and how can these diverse institutions at all levels of higher education better learn to work together for common purposes?*
- *How do we continue to educate beyond the accustomed years of early adult life, and what arrangements do we make to encourage men and women of*

> *Massachusetts to learn and to grow throughout their lives?*
> - *How can the university better serve the state in making its resources available to respond to our collective public needs?* (Alden 1971, pp. i–ii).

Wood noted that it is the responsibility of the university's trustees and executive level administration to make the decisions affecting institutional policy. However, he conceded that "we need badly to have the benefit of the detached, experienced, responsible views that you and your colleagues represent" (Alden 1971, p. ii).

The yearlong study was supported by a full-time staff of six professionals, three summer interns, and a typist. Ten external consultants and 16 scholars assisted the committee in various aspects of its work. Beyond meeting with students, faculty, administrators, and citizens, the committee surveyed half of the faculty from the Amherst campus and one-fifth of the students from the Boston campus (Alden 1971, pp. iii–iv). The result of this effort was a 124-page report which contained 28 major recommendations clustered around four topics—access, the quality and diversity of educational offerings, service to the state of Massachusetts, and institutional organization and efficiency (Alden 1971).

### An Agenda for the Eighties

Just as Wood had at the beginning of the decade, John S. Toll initiated a major planning effort when he became the University of Maryland's president in the latter part of the 1970s. Funded in large measure by the Carnegie Corporation, the two-year planning process resulted in a report that attempted to "combine outside perspective and insider knowledge" (Moos 1981, p. v). Rather than follow a strictly self-study approach or a strictly blue ribbon commission approach as the basis for an examination of institutional mission and the development of new goals, Toll brought in a special professional staff headed by Malcolm Moos, former president of the University of Minnesota, to oversee the process. In addition to the participation of 200 faculty and staff on 26 task forces, the effort utilized the services of outside consultants and a panel of nine eminent scholars from other institutions whose "marvelous and

experienced counsel helped head [the study] in the right
direction'' (pp. xiv–xv).

The University of Maryland study addressed the challenges of the 1980s with the same zeal that the Massachusetts report did regarding the challenges of the 1970s.
Many themes were the same: the need to reach minorities
and adult learners, the need to develop the newer urban
campus, the need to improve educational quality, the need
for improved administrative efficiencies, the need for
increased public service, and so forth. However, the 295-
page Maryland report was much more comprehensive and
included recommendations which most universities would
not have discussed a decade earlier. For example:

> *To grow in quality in a time of financial constraint, uni-*
> *versities need to accept the principle of substitution.*
> *That is, to race out into the academic growth fields of*
> *the 1990s, it is necessary to trim or discard some of the*
> *programs of the 1950s* (Moos 1981, p. xiii).

It recommended that the university ''concentrate more
on what it does best'' (Moos 1981, p. ix) and leave other
areas of study to other educational institutions in the state.
For example, it suggested that ''the university should
diminish those programs not connected with research
which can be taught in the state college system'' (p. 185).
To assist in the effort to establish academic priorities, the
report recommended establishing campus and system-wide
committees

> *to oversee the total configuration of academic offerings,*
> *to investigate program areas that might be condensed in*
> *the 1980s, and to pinpoint areas of future intellectual*
> *growth, public need, and importance to Maryland and*
> *its people* (Moos 1981, p. 226).

At the same time that the university was strengthening
its academic program, it should strengthen the quality of its
student body by reducing the size of the freshman class by
10 percent (a 20-percent decrease at the flagship campus
along with slight increases on the other campuses) and by
moving each campus ''toward a more selective admissions
process'' (Moos 1981, p. 213).

A number of the recommendations regarding faculty could not have been made on most campuses if the process of setting the planning agenda was solely in the hands of institutional personnel: to expand the use of faculty term appointments without tenure; to implement differential pay policies in high demand areas; to place faculty pay raises "entirely at the discretion of the university and based overwhelmingly on merit"; to place greater weight on student advising and public service in promotion and tenure decisions (Moos 1981, pp. 199–207).

## Institutional Applications

There is no apparent reason for limiting the use of blue ribbon commissions to providing national and statewide leadership. Blue ribbon commissions on the campus (and variations which involve external persons alongside institutional personnel) have made positive contributions.

Paul E. Peterson of the Brookings Institute wrote a stinging criticism of blue ribbon commissions (1983). A rapporteur for the 20th Century Fund Task Force on Federal Elementary and Secondary Education Policy (one of the many national blue ribbon panels working at the same time as the National Commission on Excellence in Education), Peterson analyzed the reports of six commissions that received wide notice, including the excellence commission. While he observes that these reports have "had a profound effect" on the national education debate, he concludes:

*This combination of factors renders commissions ill-equipped to meet the challenge of the charge.*

> *The reports themselves, upon close examination, prove to be disappointing. If we judge them by the standards ordinarily used to evaluate a policy analysis—focused statement of the problem to be analyzed, methodical evaluation of existing research, reasoned consideration of options, and presentation of supporting evidence and argumentation for well-specified proposals—they simply do not measure up. With some exceptions, the studies do not address the most difficult conceptual and political issues. Instead, they reassert what is well-known, make exaggerated claims on flimsy evidence, pontificate on matters about which there could scarcely be agreement, and make recommendations that either cost too much, cannot be implemented, or are too general to have any meaning* (Peterson 1983, p. 3).

The "inadequacies of the reports" were not the result of using poor quality commissioners, but had "to do with the nature of the commission process itself," with "the organizational and political realities of commission decision-making" (Peterson 1983, pp. 3, 9). He points out that most commissions are charged to make recommendations concerning complex problems that are not easily solvable; they are comprised of a diverse group of eminent citizens that is expected to complete its assignment with single-minded dispatch and with as little dissent as possible; and that they have no formal power. This combination of factors renders commissions ill-equipped to meet the challenge of the charge. The result is a report with a number of flaws.

## Commissions Criticized

First, commission reports generally exaggerate the problem they address. Since reports that find little to be wrong are likely to gain little public notice, a commission "is tempted to dramatize its subject matter."

> *This usually requires selective use of evidence and a profusion of strong rhetoric. Careful reasoning, balanced assessment of available information, and cautious interpretations are unlikely to survive the commission's need for public attention* (Peterson 1983, p. 9).

Second, commission reports tend to draw conclusions that are broad and general rather than specific and adventurous. In part, this is a result of the diversity of views of the commissioners. It is easier, Peterson points out, for them to agree that schools should be excellent than for them to come together on whether to limit the teaching of a certain subject because it does not contribute to quality education.

Another factor leading to broad conclusions is the broad charge given to most commissions. For example, the Business Higher Education Forum, one of the six commissions studied by Peterson, was asked "to strengthen the ability of this nation to compete more effectively in the world marketplace." In contradistinction to the National Commission on Social Security Reform that had the specific charge of recommending measures to keep the social security system from going bankrupt, education commissions work "within a much more nebulous framework" and lack "the internal capacity to define more narrow objectives that could be addressed concretely" (Peterson 1983, p. 10).

A third flaw of commission reports is that they make recommendations that are beyond the financial means of those who might implement the conclusions in the report. The sort of critical analysis and tough decision making that is associated with the ongoing duties of the commission members is not present in commission meetings, since this unpaid activity "is expected to be enjoyable and intrinsically satisfying" (Peterson 1983, p. 10).

The fourth flaw follows directly from the previous one. Since commission members do not want to get drawn into serious arguments with each other, particularly when they are not sure of the levels of acceptance that will greet their broad recommendations, they are not prone to set forth the details associated with their recommendations. Rather than argue over specific implementation issues, they leave these questions to someone else.

The setting aside of one specific "hot potato" by commissions results in the fifth flaw, Peterson says. Commissions, due to the breadth of their composition, do not find themselves able to agree on specific organizational reforms. While they might be able to agree on substantive policy proposals such as merit pay, it is difficult to gain consensus on matters requiring the rearrangement of institutional responsibilities.

Finally, Peterson finds that commission reports propose solutions that are poorly documented. Often, this is a result of understaffing, but even in those instances where the commission has an adequately-sized staff, the necessary documentation "would probably not be done" (Peterson 1983, p. 10). The commission's life cycle mitigates against it. Good staff work can be done to document the problems, but since the solutions are usually proposed at the end of the commission's existence, there is neither the time nor the desire for a detailed assessment of the recommendations. Blue ribbon commissions in education

> . . . do have their functions in American politics, but fact-finding, rigorous analysis, and policy development are usually not among them. Commissions are more appropriate for dramatizing an issue, resolving political differences, and reassuring the public that questions are being thoughtfully considered (Peterson 1983, p. 11).

**Criticisms Reconsidered**
While there may be validity to Peterson's criticisms regarding some blue ribbon commissions, the flaws that he cites are not universally true. Let us examine them one by one.

*(1) Do commissions exaggerate the problems that they address?*

Commissions are not established without a serious problem to solve, or a major task to accomplish. The real drama is in the events leading up to the establishment of the commission or in its charge. For example, the President's

Commission of Campus Unrest was established in response to a wave of student uprisings that swept the nation's campuses and culminated in the shooting of students at Kent State and Jackson State universities. President Nixon asked the commission to explain to the American people why this had happened and to suggest how to prevent its recurrence. The commission's report simply stated that campus unrest was part of a broader national condition that had begun to justify violence as a means of accomplishing a political goal. It suggested that racial injustice, the war in Vietnam, and certain campus policies had sparked the incidents of campus disquiet, and suggested that these situations needed to be remedied before such unrest would end. In the meantime, the commission suggested that dialogue be opened between students and policy makers. Exaggeration was absent.

The tone of the Commission on Campus Unrest fits its conclusion, that reconciliation should be the order of the day. However, the National Commission on Excellence in Education (1983), one of the panels critiqued by Peterson, spoke in a more dramatic tone than did the unrest commission. Nevertheless, it is difficult to conclude that it exaggerated the problem. While it may have been a bit melodramatic to assert that the American people would have "viewed the imposition of such a mediocre education system on us by a foreign power as an act of war" (p. 15), it was true that the quality of education in the nation's public schools had been spiraling precipitously downward for nearly two decades. Standardized indicators such as the College Board tests revealed that this generation's students were not achieving as much as their predecessors. Similar anecdotal complaints by employers about the poor skill levels of high school and college graduates abounded. The excellence commission did not exaggerate the problem; it merely used a few succinct and spellbinding phrases that would capture the attention of the American people.

The reports of the state-level and campus commissions do little to uphold Peterson's claim that they exaggerate the problem. The University of Massachusetts (Alden 1971), the University of Maryland (Moos 1981), and the Montana Commission (James 1974) reports tend to contradict Peterson's claim. Their citation of problems is similar to what one would find in any master plan, whether generated by a blue ribbon commission or not.

*(2) Do commissions draw conclusions that are broad and general rather than specific and adventurous?*

Among the reports of the various state-level blue ribbon commissions are sufficient data to answer this question in the negative. For example, the Final Report of the Higher Education Panel of the Commission on the Future of Education in Delaware (Smith 1977) contained recommendations in six broad areas, but went to the level of specificity in proposing 14 points that should be included in a new statute authorizing a postsecondary coordinating board. Similarly, Florida's Select Council on Posthigh School Education (Graham 1970) made 37 recommendations, including ones so specific as to propose to limit enrollments at the University of Florida and Florida State University to 26,000 full-time equivalent students, computed on a four-quarter average basis, and to propose a tuition equalization grant program to provide need-based scholarships for the difference in tuition and fee charges between the state universities and the average tuition and fee charges at Florida's independent institutions. Finally, a glance at the Final Report of the Montana Commission on Postsecondary Education (James 1974), with its 125 or so detailed recommendations, provides convincing evidence that not all commissions write nonspecific reports.

As to whether commission reports are adventurous, consider the context of the reports. Many, if not most, of the reports that established state coordinating boards, or that expanded the power of existing coordinating boards were probably adventurous for their time and place. The Wessell Commission (1975) provides clear evidence of this. Its report was so adventurous that its recommended restructuring of the State University of New York and the City University of New York was rejected. The University of Maryland report (Moos 1981) included a number of adventurous proposals; perhaps foremost was its call for a reduction in the size of the freshman class by 20 percent at the flagship campus to strengthen the quality of the student body. Since budgets are often enrollment-driven, few institutions would have the courage to entertain such a proposal.

*(3) Do commissions make recommendations that are beyond the financial means of those who would implement them?*

They probably do, but this should not be thought of in critical terms. The price tag often associated with a commission report may be high since the building of high quality, new degree programs, and the strengthening of existing programs, the implementation of financial aid programs to guarantee access to low- and middle-income students, the expansion or reconstruction of physical plants, etc., do not come cheaply. Contrary to Peterson's view that costly proposals are made so that each commissioner can get a pet project included, commissions often make their recommendations in keeping with a vision intended to move the system or the institution forward in a quantum way. Commissions are posing significant public policy questions when they recommend major expenditures, but that is what they were intended to do.

*(4) Do commissions fail to spell out the details of their proposals?*

As discussed earlier, many commission reports are very detailed.

*(5) Do commissions fail to recommend organizational changes?*

The fact that 14 of 48 gubernatorially or legislatively appointed commissions recommended either the establishment or strengthening of a state higher education agency contradicts this charge. Further organizational changes were recommended by such panels as the Wessell Commission (1975) and the Commission on the Future of the State Colleges (Cicatiello 1984) that recommended the merger of New Jersey's nine state colleges under a new central governing board.

*(6) Do commissions fail to document their proposed solutions?*

This is probably a fair criticism. While the Rosenberg Commission provided documentation regarding its recommendations, many commissions do not do so. Peterson holds that the agreement on recommendations comes so close to the end of a commission's work as to preclude documentation. But there may be another reason—some proposed solutions cannot be convincingly documented since they are contextual. For example, a proposal for a consolidated governing board (as opposed to individual boards of trustees) can be supported only in terms of the history of higher education in the particular state in question, since no one governing pattern has proven to be more successful than others. It would be difficult to prove that the location of a governing board affects institutional excellence. For example, two of our nation's leading universities are governed very differently: Berkeley is part of a central university system with a multi-institutional governing board while Michigan is independently governed by a free-standing board. Could anyone prove that either institution would be better if it adopted the governance pattern of the other? Probably not; if any change in governance were recommended by a commission for an institution, it would be based not on documentable data, but on the political and/or economic context of the state at the time of the recommendation.

**Using Commissions**
Based on a broad examination of blue ribbon commissions, one must conclude that they can and do make proposals that are detailed, forward-looking, and often controversial. They can be used effectively in the following circumstances:

(1) when it becomes important to bring the academy into conformance with societal needs;
(2) when a group of eminent citizens can lend its prestige toward solving a complex problem;
(3) when it is necessary to make an uncertain future more certain;
(4) when internal groups are too divided to resolve an issue;
(5) when an organization does not have the power to effect a desirable change;
(6) when a fresh view and bold new ideas are desired.

These occasions often occur at the national, state, and institutional levels. Units within a college or university also can benefit from the use of blue ribbon commissions. For example, a chemistry department may want to revise its curriculum to ensure that its students are appropriately prepared for the sorts of jobs that will exist in the coming 5-10 years. A blue ribbon panel comprised of high-level persons from the chemical and pharmaceutical industries, representatives of federal or state environmental protection and labor market forecasting units, and scholars from other institutions would be very helpful in identifying areas for departmental growth and consolidation.

**Effective Commissions**

To be effective, blue ribbon commissions must have the following characteristics:

(1) the membership should include eminent citizens and should be reflective of a broad range of views and interests;
(2) the charge to the commission must be clear and comprehensive;
(3) the commission should hold enough meetings for its members to understand fully the issues at hand and the various solutions under consideration;
(4) the commission's chair must provide strong leadership;
(5) the commission's staff must be knowledgeable and appropriate in number to provide the necessary background research;
(6) the commission should seek public opinion concerning the various problems and solutions under study;
(7) the commission's report must address the objectives set forth in the charge, provide adequate documentation of the problems, make recommendations that have a clear relationship to the problems and that are readily understandable, provide documentation concerning the recommendations when possible;
(8) the members of the commission must be willing to advocate on behalf of their report once it is issued.

Commissions that follow these rules have the potential to provide a great service. The involvement of a distinguished group of outsiders can provide a higher education system or institution with both a fresh view and a "reality check.'' Commissions can be a masterful means of developing consensus, and also can be the instrument through which bold policy initiatives are given a legitimate place on the agenda of the academy.

# REFERENCES

The ERIC Clearinghouse on Higher Education abstracts and indexes the current literature on higher education for the Office of Educational Research and Improvement's monthly bibliographic journal, *Resources in Education*. Most of these publications are available through the ERIC Document Reproduction Service (EDRS). For publications cited in this bibliography that are available from EDRS, ordering number and price are included. Readers who wish to order a publication should write to the ERIC Document Reproduction Service, 3900 Wheeler Avenue, Alexandria, Virginia, 22304. When ordering, please specify the document number. Documents are available as noted in microfiche (MF) and paper copy (PC). Because prices are subject to change, it is advisable to check the latest issue of *Resources in Education* for current cost based on the number of pages in the publication.

Ad Hoc Committee on Community College Governance. January 1968. "Report." Salem, Oreg.: Oregon Educational Coordinating Council.

Ad Hoc Committee on Private and Independent Higher Education. October 1968. "State Assistance to Private and Independent Higher Education in Oregon." Salem, Oreg.: Oregon Educational Coordinating Council. ED 031 997. 84 pp. MF–$0.97; PC–$9.36.

Alaska House Committee on Health, Education, and Social Services and Finance. 1977a. "An Act Creating the University of Alaska Fiscal Management Committee and Providing for an Effective Date." Mimeographed. H.R. No. 360. 10th leg., 1st sess. Juneau, Ala.: House of Representatives.

———. 1977b. "Creating an Interim Oversight Committee for Review of Business Management Practices and Fiscal Procedures of the University of Alaska." Mimeographed. H.R. No. 36, 10th leg., 1st sess. Juneau, Ala.: House of Representatives.

———. 1978. "An Act Creating the University of Alaska Structure and Fiscal Review Committee and Providing for an Effective Date." Mimeographed. Substitute for N.R. No. 666, 10th leg., 2nd sess. Juneau, Ala.: House of Representatives.

Alden, Vernon R. 1971. "Report of the President's Committee on the Future University of Massachusetts." Boston: University of Massachusetts.

Armstrong, Edward H. October 1975. "Report on the Committee on Governance. For Master Plan Phase IV." Springfield, Ill.: Illinois State Board of Higher Education. ED 129 126. 91 pp. MF–$10.97; PC–$9.36.

Berg, Ivan. 1981. "Report of the Blue Ribbon Panel on Teacher Education." Mimeographed. Trenton, N.J.: Department of Higher Education.

Blackburn, J. Gilmer. March 1979. "Alabama's Challenge: Higher Education for the 1980's. Report of the Second Special Committee to Evaluate the Alabama Commission on Higher Education." Montgomery, Ala.: Alabama State Commission on Higher Education. ED 169 823. 74 pp. MF–$0.97; PC–$7.16.

Booher, Edward E. 1976a. "An Analysis of the Family Income of Full-Time Collegiate Students in New Jersey." Mimeographed. Trenton: New Jersey State Commission on Financing Postsecondary Education. ED 129 164. 29 pp. MF–$0.97; PC–$5.34.

———. 1976b. "An Analysis of the Monetary Benefits and Costs of Higher Education in New Jersey in 1975–1976." Mimeographed. Trenton: New Jersey State Commission on Financing Postsecondary Education. ED 125 471. 55 pp. MF–$0.97; PC–$7.14.

———. 1976c. "Interstate Comparisons of Higher Education Systems in Nine States." Trenton: New Jersey State Commission on Financing Postsecondary Education. ED 222 121. 78 pp. MF–$0.97; PC–$9.36.

———. 1976d. "Student Resource Survey of Selected New Jersey Residents Attending College in Another State." Mimeographed. Trenton: New Jersey State Commission on Financing Postsecondary Education. ED 129 165. 41 pp. MF–$0.97; PC–$5.34.

———. February 1977a. "An Analysis of New Jersey Postsecondary Education Expenditures: The Current System (FY76) and the Commission Recommendations." Trenton: New Jersey State Commission on Financing Postsecondary Education. ED 222 129. 89 pp. MF–$0.97; PC $9.36.

———. 1977b. "Equity and County College Financing." Mimeographed. Trenton: New Jersey State Commission on Financing Postsecondary Education. ED 176 809. 68 pp. MF–$0.97; PC–$7.14.

———. 1977c. "Financing in an Era of Uncertainty. Final Report." Trenton: New Jersey State Commission on Financing Postsecondary Education. ED 148 195. 221 pp. MF–$0.97; PC–$16.20.

———. 1977d. "Undergraduate Enrollment Projections for New Jersey Institutions of Postsecondary Education, 1976–1990." Trenton: New Jersey State Commission on Financing Postsecondary Education. ED 129 161. 34 pp. MF–$0.97; PC–$5.34.

Booz, Allen, and Booz, Hamilton. 1972. "Review of Alternatives for Medical Education in North Dakota." Mimeographed. Chicago.

Browder, William. 1975. "Illinois Board of Higher Education Committee to Study Public Community College Financing." Mimeographed. Springfield, Ill.: Board of Higher Education.

Brunsen, William H. October 1976a. "Working Paper II on the Coordinating of Higher Education for the L.R. 36 Interim Study Committee." Mimeographed. Lincoln, Nebr.: Legislative Fiscal Analyst Committee.

―――. November 1976b. "Working Paper III on the Coordinating of Higher Education for the L.R. 36 Interim Study Committee." Lincoln, Nebr.: Legislative Fiscal Analyst Committee.

Bureau of Research, Planning, and Evaluation. 1977a. "Purposes of Postsecondary Education: Commissioner's Recommended Statement." Providence, R.I.: Department of Education.

―――. 1977b. "Purposes of Postsecondary Education Planning Project; Project Summary." Mimeographed. Providence, R.I.: Department of Education.

Burnes, Donald; Johnson, Janet R.; Palaich, Robert; and Flakus-Mosqueda, Patricia. 1982. "Setting Up Blue Ribbon Commissions." *E.C.S. Issuegram #15.* Denver, Colo. Education Commission of the States. ED 234 503. 10 pp. MF–$0.97; PC–$3.54.

Bussis, Dale. 1969. "Higher Education in Vermont: Its Resources and Needs: A Report to the Vermont Commission on Higher Education Facilities." New York: Institute for Educational Development. ED 032 825. 108 pp. MF–$0.97; PC–$11.16.

California Legislature. 1973. "Assembly Bill No. 770, 1973–74 Regular Session, 15 March 1973." Mimeographed. Sacramento, Calif.: State Assembly of California.

California State Postsecondary Education Commission. January 1979. "Postcommission Final Draft: Recommendations of Interest to Commission." Sacramento, Calif.: California State Postsecondary Education. ED 222 138. 7 pp. MF–$0.97; PC–$3.54.

Carnegie Commission on Higher Education. 1973. "Priorities for Action: Final Report of the Carnegie Commission on Higher Education." New York: McGraw-Hill.

Carnegie Foundation for the Advancement of Teaching. Panel on Government and Higher Education. 1982. "The Control of the Campus: A Report on the Governance of Higher Education." Washington, D.C.: Carnegie Foundation.

Citizens Advisory Committee on Graduate Education. March 1978. "Report on Graduate Education in Oregon." Report No. 78-00A. Eugene: Oregon State Board of Higher Education. ED 222 126. 88 pp. MF–$0.97; PC–$9.36.

Coles, James S. 1967. "Report of the Advisory Commission for the Higher Education Study to the Honorable Kenneth M. Curtis, Governor of Maine, and the Legislature of the State of Maine." Mimeographed. Augusta, Maine.

Commission on the Organization of the Government of the District of Columbia. 1972. "Report, Vol. I. Summary." Washington: U.S. Government Printing Office.

Connecticut. 1977. "Public Act No. 77-573: An Act Reorganizing Higher Education." Substitute House Bill No. 7658. Mimeographed. Hartford: State Legislature.

Coons, Arthur G. 1960. "A Master Plan for Higher Education in California, 1960–1975." Sacramento: California State Department of Education. ED 011 193. 249 pp. MF–$0.97; PC–$20.99.

Council of the District of Columbia. November 1975. "The District of Columbia Public Postsecondary Education Reorganization Act Amendments." Mimeographed Notice. D.C. Law No. 1-36. Washington.

Crosby, Harold Bryan. 1976. "Access to Knowledge: Vol. 1, Preliminary Report of the Florida Commission on Educational Outreach and Service." Tallahassee: State University System of Florida.

Educational Television and Radio Advisory Committee to the Oregon Educational Coordinating Commission. 1976. "Educational Telecommunications in Oregon." Eugene: Oregon Educational Coordinating Commission.

Erickson, Emil. 1979. "Report to the Governor and 1979 Minnesota Legislature by the Minnesota Higher Education Coordinating Board." St. Paul: Minnesota Higher Education Coordinating Board.

Eurich, Alvin C. 1976. "Looking Ahead to Better Education in Missouri." Mimeographed. Jefferson City, Mo.: Consultant Panel.

Finnegan, Francis, T. May 1973. "Advisory Commission for the Study of Public Support for Postsecondary Education in Maine." Augusta: Maine State Advisory Commission for the Study of Public Support for Postsecondary Education. ED 222 134. 94 pp. MF–$0.97; PC–$9.36.

Fleming, Arthur. 1982. "Final Report to Chancellor T. Edward Hollander." Trenton, N.J.: Department of Higher Education.

Friday, William C. 1983. "Report of the Commission on the Future of North Carolina: Goals and Recommendations for the Year 2000." Chapel Hill: Commission on the Future of North Carolina.

Gardner, David P. 1983. "A Nation at Risk: The Imperative for Educational Reform." Washington, D.C.: U.S. Department of Education, National Commission on Excellence in Education. ED 226 006. 72 pp. MF–$0.97; PC–$7.14.

Glenny, Lyman A. 1967. "Long-Range Planning for State Educational Needs. Seven Crucial Issues in Education: Alternatives for State Action." Denver, Colo.: Education Commission of the States.

————. January 1972. "The Anonymous Leaders of Higher Education." *Journal of Higher Education* 43: 18.

————. Berdahl, Robert O.; Palola, Ernest G.; and Paltridge, James G. 1971. "Coordinating Higher Education for the '70s." Berkeley, Calif.: The Center for Research and Development in Higher Education, University of California. ED 057 752. 108 pp. MF–$0.97; PC–$10.74.

Glynn, Edward. 1981. "Autonomy and Accountability in Higher Education." The Report of the Commission on Educational Accountability. Trenton, N.J.: Department of Higher Education.

Goheen, Robert F. 1965. "A Call to Action." Princeton: Citizen's Committee for Higher Education in New Jersey.

Gove, Samuel K., and Zollinger, Richard A., eds. 1979. "Final Report of the President's Assembly on State Policy Research at the University of Illinois." Urbana: University of Illinois.

Governor's Committee on Postsecondary Education. 1982a. "Maintaining Progress in Georgia Postsecondary Education. Recommendations for Today; Concerns for Tomorrow." Atlanta: Author. ED 230 121. 39 pp. MF–$0.97; PC–$5.34.

————, March 1982b. "New Directions for Student Aid in Georgia." Atlanta: Author. ED 217 765. 20 pp. MF–$0.97.

Governor's Council for Cost Control. 1977. "What Price Education: An Overview of Problems Facing Ohio's Higher Education System and Their Impact on the Taxpayer." Columbus.

————. April 1978. "College: The Coming Crisis. An Analysis of How Major Trends in Ohio's Higher Education System Will Affect the Role of Two-Year Colleges." Mimeographed. Columbus.

Graham, D. Robert. 1970. "Florida Posthigh–School Education: A Comprehensive Plan for the 70's. A Report on Public and Independent Posthigh-School Education in Florida to the Florida Legislature." Tallahassee: Select Council on Posthigh-School Education. ED 041 468. 92 pp. MF–$0.97; PC–$9.36.

Gray, John E. January 1969. "Challenge for Excellence: A Blueprint for Progress in Higher Education." Mimeographed. Austin: Coordinating Board of Texas University and College System. ED 030 368. 45 pp. MF–$0.97; PC–$5.34.

Haley, Fred T. 1969. "Temporary Committee on Educational Policies, Structure, and Management." Mimeographed. Olympia, Wash.

Hamerlinck, Donald. 1977. "Report to the 1977 Minnesota Legislature by the Minnesota Higher Education Coordinating Board." Mimeographed. St. Paul: Minnesota Higher Education

Coordinating Board. ED 138 138. 210 pp. MF–$0.97; PC–$16.20.

Hardin, Taylor. 1983. "Report of the Council of Twenty-One: Challenge—Obligation—Opportunity: The Imperative for Excellence in Higher Education." Montgomery: Alabama Commission on Higher Education.

Hausauer, LeRoy. 1979. "Report of the North Dakota Legislative Council. Forty Sixth Legislative Assembly, 1979." Bismarck: North Dakota Legislative Council.

Howard, John. 1974. "Coordination of Postsecondary Education in Oregon." Salem: Oregon Educational Coordinating Council.

James, Ted. 1974. "Final Report: Montana Commission on Postsecondary Education." Helena: Commission on Postsecondary Education.

Johnson, Janet Rogers–Clarke, June 1982. "Perceptions of Factors Affecting the Relative Effectiveness of Temporary Blue Ribbon State Commissions." Ph.D. Dissertation. University of Denver. ED 222 160. 220 pp. MF–$0.97; PC–$16.20.

Johnson, John V. 1981. "Commission to Study Teacher Preparation Programs." Final Report. Trenton, N.J.: Department of Higher Education.

Kernes, Otto. 1968. *Report of the National Advisory Commission on Civil Disorders*. New York: Bantam Books.

Kitchel, Douglas. 1968. "Higher Education in Vermont: Report of the Committee to Study Proposal No. 23." Mimeographed. Montpelier: Legislative Council.

Kohler, Walter. 1969. "Academic Plan for Wisconsin's Public Universities, 1970–1980." Madison: Wisconsin Coordinating Council for Higher Education. ED 037 154. 88 pp. MF–$0.97; PC–$9.36.

Kroening, Carl W. 1975. "Making the Transition: Report to the 1975 Minnesota Legislature." Mimeographed. St. Paul: Minnesota Higher Education Coordinating Commission. ED 102 892. 128 pp. MF–$0.97; PC–$10.80.

Legislative Program Review and Investigations Committee. 1977. "Strengthening Higher Education in Connecticut." Hartford: Legislative Program Review and Investigations Committee. ED 138 163. 91 pp. MF–$0.97; PC–$9.36.

Lierheimer, Alvin P. December 1977/January 1978. "A Closer Look at Higher Education Governance." *Inside Education:* 6–7: 14.

Little, Arthur D., and Rumsey, William H. 1972. "Summary Report to the District of Columbia Government: A Comprehensive Plan for Public Higher Education in the District of Columbia." Cambridge, Mass.: Arthur D. Little, Inc.

Lynch, Jack C. 1973. "Responding to Change: Recommended State Policy for Meeting Minnesota's Present and Future Needs for Postsecondary Education." Mimeographed. St. Paul: Minnesota Higher Education Coordinating Commission. ED 074 945. 219 pp. MF–$0.97; PC–$16.20.

Mahoney, Eugene T. 1976. "The Second Interim Report of the Legislative Resolution 36 Interim Study Committee on Postsecondary Education." Mimeographed. Lincoln, NE.

Marcus, Laurence R.; Leone, Anita O., and Goldberg, Edward D. 1983. "The Path to Excellence: Quality Assurance in Higher Education." ASHE-ERIC. Higher Education Research Report No. 1. Washington, D.C.; American Association for Higher Education. ED 227 800. 76 pp. MF–$0.97; PC–$9.36.

Maurer, Lucille. 1976. "Planning for New Directions in Education: The Rosenberg Commission." *The University of Maryland Forum* 6(1): 21–25.

McCain, James A. 1966a. "The First Business of Our Times: A Report to the Advisory Commission for the Higher Education Study, State of Maine." Mimeographed. Augusta.

————. 1966b. "Meeting Maine's Basic Responsibilities for Higher Education. A Special Report to the Maine State Board of Education." Mimeographed. Augusta.

McLean Associates. 1973. "Higher Education in Alaska; A Report Based Upon Follow-up Visits to Sitka College and Ankorage." Mimeographed. Juneau, Ala.

————. 1974. "Higher Education in Alaska; A Report with Special Reference to the Community Colleges." Mimeographed. Juneau, Ala.

————. 1975. "Higher Education in Alaska 1974–1975." Juneau, Ala.

————. 1976. "Higher Education in Alaska 1975–1976. Submitted to the Subcommittee on Higher Education of the Legislative Council, 9th Alaska Legislature (1975–1976)." Juneau, Ala.: Author. ED 222 127. 173 pp. MF–$0.97; PC–$15.17.

Melland, Robert. 1977. "Report of the North Dakota Legislative Council, Forty-Fifth Legislative Assembly, 1977." Bismarck: North Dakota Legislative Council.

————. 1982. "Higher Education Study Commission." Bismarck: Higher Education Study Commission.

Millard, R. M. December 1977. "Statewide Coordination and Governance of Postsecondary Education: Quality, Costs, and Accountability—the Major Issues of the 1980s." Seminar on Statewide Coordination and Governance of Postsecondary Education. Wayzata, Minn.: Spring Hill Center. ED 202 318. 23 pp. MF–$0.97; PC–$3.54.

Mississippi Select Committee for Higher Education." 1974.
"Final Report." Mimeographed. Jackson, Miss.

Missouri Governor's Conference on Education Committee. 1968.
"Planning and Financing Education for the Future: A Report
for the Missouri Governor's Conference on Education." Mimeographed. Columbia, Mo.

Missouri Governor's Task Force on the Role of Private Higher
Education. 1970. "The Tucker Report." Jefferson City.

Missouri State Extension Study Commission. March 1978.
"Report to the Governor and General Assembly." Jefferson
City, Mo. ED 222 130. 132 pp. MF–$0.97; PC–$12.96.

Moos, Malcolm. 1981. "The Post-Land Grant University: The
University of Maryland Report." Adelphi, Md.: University of
Maryland.

Murray, J. Terence. 1982. "Strategic Development Commission." Providence, R.I.: Strategic Development Commission.

National Advisory Committee on Education. 1931. "Federal
Relations to Education, Part I." Washington, D.C.: National
Capital Press.

National Commission on Excellence in Education. 1983. *A
Nation at Risk: The Imperative for Educational Reform*. Washington, D.C.: U.S. Government Printing Office. ED 226 006. 72
pp. MF–$0.97; PC–$7.14.

Newman, Frank. 1971. *Report on Higher Education*. Washington, D.C.: U.S. Government Printing Office. ED 049 718. 136
pp. MF–$0.97; PC–$11.16.

O'Brien, Anna Belle, C. 1982. "The Tennessee Comprehensive
Education Study: A Task Force Review of Public Education."
Nashville: Comprehensive Education Study Task Force. ED
228 711. 622 pp. MF–$1.27; PC–$45.00.

Oregon Legislative Research. 1973. "Legislative Staffing." Mimeographed. Eugene, Oreg.

Ortiz, Edward A. 1982. "A Statewide Plan for Postsecondary
Education in New Mexico: 1983–1987." Santa Fe: State of
New Mexico Commission on Postsecondary Education.

Peck, Robert. 1971. "Comprehensive Education Planning in Oregon." Salem, Oreg.: Oregon Education Coordinating Council.

Pelisek, Frank. April 1975. "President's Report in Response to
the Governor's Request on Reducing the Scope of the University of Wisconsin System." Madison: Board of Regents, University of Wisconsin. ED 222 140. 103 pp. MF–$0.97; PC–
$11.16.

Peterson, Paul E. Winter 1983. "Did the Education Commissions
Say Anything? *Brookings Review*. 3–11 pp.

Platt, Joseph B. 1972. "The California Master Plan for Higher
Education in the Seventies and Beyond; Report and Recom-

mendations of the Select Committee on the Master Plan for Higher Education to the Coordinating Council for Higher Education." Sacramento: Select Committee. ED 071 567. 158 pp. MF–$0.97; PC–$12.60.

Post-High School Study Committee. 1966. "Education Beyond the High School, A Projection for Oregon." Salem, Oreg.: Oregon Educational Coordinating Council.

Prichard, Edward F., Jr. October 1981. "In Pursuit of Excellence: The Report of the Prichard Committee on Higher Education in Kentucky's Future to the Kentucky Council on Higher Education." Frankfort: Ky.: Council on Public Higher Education. ED 214 442. 152 pp. MF–$0.97; PC–$16.17.

Race, George J. 1982. "Governor's Task Force on Higher Education—Report and Recommendations." Austin, Tex.: Governor's Task Force.

Reed, Donald H., Jr. 1978. "Commission on the Future of Florida's Public Universities." Tallahassee: Commission on the Future of Florida's Public Universities. ED 222 122. 81 pp. MF–$0.97; PC–$9.36.

Rosenberg, Leonard H. 1975. "Final Report of the Governor's Commission on Education." Baltimore: Governor's Study Commission on Structure and Governance of Education for Maryland. ED 112 710. 58 pp. MF–$0.97; PC–$7.14.

Rosenthal, Alan. Winter 1977. "The Emerging Legislative Role in Education." *Compact* 11:(1)2. Denver, Colo.: Education Commission of the States.

Sava, Samuel. 1974. "Final Report: Citizens' Task Force on Higher Education." Columbus, Ohio: Citizen's Task Force.

Scranton, William W. 1970. *Report of the President's Commission on Campus Unrest*. Washington, D.C.: U.S. Government Printing Office. ED 083 899. 419 pp. MF–$0.97; PC–$30.60.

Seidman, L. William. 1974a. "Interim Report." Mimeographed. Lansing: Governor's Commission on Higher Education.

——— . 1974b. "Building for the Future of Postsecondary Education in Michigan." Mimeographed. Lansing: Governor's Commission on Higher Education. ED 080 205. 71 pp. MF–$0.97; PC–$7.14.

Sevilla, Carlos. November 1976. "Report on State Services to the Hispanic Population of Wisconsin." Madison: Governor's Council for Spanish Speaking People. ED 222 139. 135 pp. MF–$0.97; PC–$12.96.

Silver, Ann. 1982. "Report by the Governor's Task Force on Employment Training." Carson City, Nev.: Governor's Task Force.

Singer, Paul L. August 1973. "University of Arizona, College of Medicine Admissions Review Committee." Phoenix. Ariz.: Board of Regents. ED 222 124. 20 pp. MF–$0.97; PC–$3.54.

Sloan Commission on Government and Higher Education. 1980. *A Program for Renewed Partnerships. The Report of the Sloan Commission on Government and Higher Education.* Cambridge, Mass.: Ballinger Publishing Company.

Smallwood, Frank. 1971. "Higher Education in Vermont; Past, Present and Future." Mimeographed. Burlington, Vt.: Joint Committee on Higher Education Planning.

Smith, Kenneth M. August 1977a. "Charge to the Commission on the Future of Education in Delaware." Memorandum. Wilmington, Del.

———. 1977b. "Final Report." Dover: Delaware State Commission on the Future of Education. ED 222 135. 9 pp. ED–$0.97; PC–$3.54.

Smith, William Reece, Jr. 1980. "Report and Recommendations of the Joint Legislative and Executive Commission on Postsecondary Education." Tallahassee, Fla.: Joint Legislative and Executive Commission.

Streibel, Bryce. 1975. "Report of the North Dakota Legislative Council, Forty-Fourth Legislative Assembly, 1975." Bismarck: North Dakota Legislative Council.

Sutton, Richard L. December 1976. "Report to the Governor and General Assembly of the State of Delaware by the Governor's Higher Education Advisory Commission." Dover: Delaware State Higher Education Advisory Commission. ED 222 136. 7 pp. MF–$0.97; PC–$3.54.

Taylor, Robert H. 1977. "Excellence and the Open Door: An Essential Partnership. A Report of the Commission to Study the Mission, Financing, and Governance of the County Colleges, State of New Jersey." Trenton: Department of Higher Education. ED 167 217. 72 pp. MF–$0.97; PC–$8.94.

Thomas, DeRoy C. 1982. "Report of the Governor's Commission on Higher Education and the Economy." Hartfort, Conn.: Governor's Commission. ED 216 623. 150 pp. MF–$0.97; PC–$12.96.

University of Wisconsin System. 1975a. "Report of the Economic Impact Committee, System Advisory Planning Task Force: The Economic and Fiscal Consequences of Reducing the Scope of the University of Wisconsin System, Phase II." Madison: System Advisory Planning Task Force.

———. 1975b. "Report of the System Advisory Planning Task Force, Book I; Reducing the Scope of the University of Wisconsin System: Planning for the 1980 Analyses, Criteria, Simulation Studies." Madison: System Advisory Planning Task Force.

Vermont Governor's Blue Ribbon Commission on Higher Education. November 1973. "Interim Report: Governor's Blue Ribbon Commission on Higher Education." Montpelier: Author. ED 222 163. 8 pp. MF–$0.97.

Vermont Technical Education Commission. January 1969. "Vermont Technical Education Commission Report." Montpelier. Author. ED 222 132. 20 pp. MF–$0.97; PC–$3.54.

Warner, Jerome. December 1976a. "A Proposal for Legislative Coordination of Postsecondary Education in Nebraska." Lincon: Legislative Resolution 36 Interim Study Committee.

———. 1976b. "A Report of the Legislative Resolution 36 Interim Study Committee to the Members of the Nebraska Legislative Council." Lincoln: Legislative Resolution 36.

Washington State Temporary Advisory Council on Public Higher Education. January 1969. "Report on Higher Education in Washington." Olympia. ED 222 133. 22 pp. MF–$0.97; PC–$3.54.

Wells, Harry K. 1976. "Twelfth Annual Report and Recommendations of the Maryland Council for Higher Education." Annapolis: Maryland Council for Higher Education. ED 121 206. 114 pp. MF–$0.97; PC–$11.16.

———. 1978a. "Maryland Public and Private Postsecondary Institutions, Agencies, and Boards Directory." Mimeographed. Annapolis: State Postsecondary Education Commission.

———. 1978b. "Maryland Statewide Plan for Postsecondary Education July 1978." Annapolis: State Postsecondary Education Commission.

Wessell, Nils, Y. 1976. "Preliminary Report of the Temporary State Commission on Postsecondary Education." Albany, N.Y.: Temporary State Commission.

———. 1977a. "Preliminary Report of the Major Recommendations of the Temporary State Commission on the Future of Postsecondary Education in New York State." Albany: Temporary State Commission.

———. 1977b. "Report of the Temporary State Commission on the Future of Postsecondary Education in New York State." Albany: Temporary State Commission.

Whiteman, Jack W. February 1977. "A Report to the Thirty-Third Legislature, State of Arizona, on the Feasibility of Establishing a Branch of Arizona State University in Western Maricopa County." Phoenix: Arizona Governor's Office. ED 222 125. 47 pp. MF–$0.97; PC–$5.34.

Wilner, Alan M. December 1975. "Report and Recommendations of the Task Force to Evaluate the Final Report of the Governor's Study Commission on Structure and Governance of Education." Annapolis, Md.: Maryland Governor's Study Commission. ED 222 123. 25 pp. MF–$0.97.

Zachry, H. B. August 1964. "Education: Texas' Resource for Tomorrow. Report of the Governor's Committee on Education Beyond the High School." Mimeographed. Austin: Texas Governor's Committee. ED 222 137. 16 pp. MF–$0.97; PC–$3.54.

# INDEX

**A**

Access to education, 5, 19, 23–24, 41
Accountability demands, 26
Adult education, 19, 25
Affirmative action, 6, 26, 56–58
Alabama
    commission effectiveness, 29–30
    commission membership, 13
    Education Study Commission, 29
Alaska
    commission membership, 13
    consultant service use, 13
Alden, Vernon R., 50
American Indians, 24
Areas of authority/recommendations, 15, 19, 22, 24
Arizona
    branch campus expansion, 13, 23
    commission membership, 13
    Legislature, 13, 25
    Medical School Admissions Review Committee, 25
Arizona State University, 13, 25
Authority/charge given, 12, 30–31, 66

**B**

Block grants, 4
Blue Ribbon Panel on Teacher Education (NJ), 16
Board-college relationship, 58
Branch campus expansion, 13, 23, 25
Bundy aid program, 41
Business Higher Education Forum, 66
Business sector relationships, 55

**C**

California
    commission membership, 13
    master planning, 24
    state coordinating agency special study, 19
Cambodian invasion, 5
Campus-based commissions, 55–63
Campus violence, 4–5, 66
Carey, Hugh, 38
Carnegie Commission on Higher Education, 6, 7, 9
Carnegie Corporation, 61
Carnegie Foundation for the Advancement of Learning, 8
Carter, Jimmy, 4
Change strategies, 11

## L

Lay persons as members, 13, 38
Leadership role
      commission chairman, 46, 72
      regional, 55
Legislative appointment, 12, 19
Legislators as members, 13, 45
Louisiana: commission membership, 13
Lucey, Patrick, 59


## M

Maine
      consultant service use, 13
      student financial aid, 24
Mississippi State Police, 4
Missouri: financing education, 23
Montana
      Commission on Postsecondary Education, 24, 68, 69
      governance issues, 23
      master planning, 24
Moos, Malcolm, 61
Multicampus institutions, 59–60


## N

National Advisory Committee on Education, 3, 9
National Commission on Excellence in Education, 3, 65, 68
National Commission on Social Security Reform, 66
National Panel on Government and Higher Education, 8, 9
National survey of commissions, 17–25
Nationally oriented commissions (see Federal commissions)
Nebraska: commission membership, 13
New Jersey
      affirmative action case, 56
      Blue Ribbon Panel on Teacher Education, 16
      Board of Higher Education, 15
      Citizens Committee for Higher Education, 15
      Commission on the Future of the State Colleges, 16, 70
      Commission to Study Teacher Preparation Programs, 16
      Commission to Study the Mission, Financing and Governance of County Colleges (NJ), 16
      governance issues, 23
      merger of state colleges, 70
      seven higher education panels, 15–16
      student financial aid, 24
New York (see also Wessell Commission)
      State Legislature, 41

# ASHE-ERIC HIGHER EDUCATION REPORTS

Starting in 1983, the Association for the Study of Higher Education assumed cosponsorship of the Higher Education Reports with the ERIC Clearinghouse on Higher Education. For the previous 11 years, ERIC and the American Association for Higher Education prepared and published the reports.

Each report is the definitive analysis of a tough higher education problem, based on a thorough research of pertinent literature and institutional experiences. Report topics, identified by a national survey, are written by noted practitioners and scholars with prepublication manuscript reviews by experts.

Eight monographs (10 monographs before 1985) in the ASHE-ERIC Higher Education Report series are published each year, available individually or by subscription. Subscription to eight issues is $60 regular; $50 for members of AERA, AAHE and AIR: $40 for members of ASHE. (Add $7.50 outside the United States.)

Prices for single copies, including 4th class postage and handling, are $10.00 regular and $7.50 for members of AERA, AAHE, AIR, and ASHE ($7.50 regular and $6.00 for members for 1983 and 1984 reports, $6.50 regular and $5.00 for members for reports published before 1983). If faster 1st class postage is desired for U.S. and Canadian orders, add $.75 for each publication ordered: overseas, add $4.50. For VISA and MasterCard payments, include card number, expiration date, and signature. Orders under $25 must be prepaid. Bulk discounts are available on orders of 15 or more reports (not applicable to subscriptions). Order from the Publications Department, Association for the Study of Higher Education, One Dupont Circle, Suite 630, Washington, D.C. 20036, 202/296-2597. Write for a publication list of all the Higher Education Reports available.

## 1986 Higher Education Reports

1. Post-tenure Faculty Evaluation: Threat or Opportunity?
   *Christine M. Licata*

2. Blue Ribbon Commissions and Higher Education: Changing Academe from the Outside
   *Janet R. Johnson and Laurence R. Marcus*

## 1985 Higher Education Reports

1. Flexibility in Academic Staffing: Effective Policies and Practices
   *Kenneth P. Mortimer, Marque Bagshaw, and Andrew T. Masland*

2. Associations in Action: The Washington, D.C., Higher Education Community
   *Harland G. Bloland*

3. And on the Seventh Day: Faculty Consulting and Supplemental Income
   *Carol M. Boyer and Darrell R. Lewis*

4. Faculty Research Performance: Lessons from the Sciences and Social Sciences
   *John W. Creswell*

5. Academic Program Reviews: Institutional Approaches, Expectations, and Controversies
   *Clifton F. Conrad and Richard F. Wilson*

6. Students in Urban Settings: Achieving the Baccalaureate Degree
   *Richard C. Richardson, Jr., and Louis W. Bender*

7. Serving More Than Students: A Critical Need for College Student Personnel Services
   *Peter H. Garland*

8. Faculty Participation in Decision Making: Necessity or Luxury?
   *Carol E. Floyd*

### 1984 Higher Education Reports

1. Adult Learning: State Policies and Institutional Practices
   *K. Patricia Cross and Anne-Marie McCartan*

2. Student Stress: Effects and Solutions
   *Neal A. Whitman, David C. Spendlove, and Claire H. Clark*

3. Part-time Faculty: Higher Education at a Crossroads
   *Judith M. Gappa*

4. Sex Discrimination Law in Higher Education: The Lessons of the Past Decade
   *J. Ralph Lindgren, Patti T. Ota, Perry A. Zirkel, and Nan Van Gieson*

5. Faculty Freedoms and Institutional Accountability: Interactions and Conflicts
   *Steven G. Olswang and Barbara A. Lee*

6. The High-Technology Connection: Academic/Industrial Cooperation for Economic Growth
   *Lynn G. Johnson*

7. Employee Educational Programs: Implications for Industry and Higher Education
   *Suzanne W. Morse*

8. Academic Libraries: The Changing Knowledge Centers of Colleges and Universities
   *Barbara B. Moran*

9. Futures Research and the Strategic Planning Process: Implications for Higher Education
   *James L. Morrison, William L. Renfro, and Wayne I. Boucher*

10. Faculty Workload: Research, Theory, and Interpretation
    *Harold E. Yuker*

### 1983 Higher Education Reports

1. The Path to Excellence: Quality Assurance in Higher Education
   *Laurence R. Marcus, Anita O. Leone, and Edward D. Goldberg*

2. Faculty Recruitment, Retention, and Fair Employment: Obligations and Opportunities
   *John S. Waggaman*

3. Meeting the Challenges: Developing Faculty Careers
   *Michael C. T. Brookes and Katherine L. German*

4. Raising Academic Standards: A Guide to Learning Improvement
   *Ruth Talbott Keimig*